Enjoy your ride!

4/6/08

On the Back
of
a Buffalo

Eastern Stories for Western Journey

Interfaith Dialogue

Nobuaki Hanaoka
Foreword by Alfred Bloom

ISBN 0-7414-4391-0

Published by:

INFINITY
PUBLISHING.COM

1094 New DeHaven Street, Suite 100
West Conshohocken, PA 19428-2713
Info@buybooksontheweb.com
www.buybooksontheweb.com
Toll-free (877) BUY BOOK
Local Phone (610) 941-9999
Fax (610) 941-9959

Printed in the United States of America

Printed on Recycled Paper

Published December 2007

Acknowledgments

I am truly grateful to all those who have inspired me to write this book. Among them is Dr. Paul Nagano, my mentor in pastoral ministry and a great friend for many years. He has repeatedly challenged me to embrace my Eastern spiritual and cultural heritage in my theological pursuits. Dr. Alfred Bloom, an internationally renowned Buddhist scholar, was kind enough to take the time to read the manuscript. He gave me some invaluable suggestions and wrote the foreword to the book. He has indeed been an inspiration to me, particularly in the area of Buddhist-Christian dialogue, and a great friend, as well. Ms. Patricia Heinicke, another good friend, was the one who originally encouraged me to put some of the Eastern stories I used in my sermons when I was pastor at Epworth United Methodist Church in Berkeley, California into a book form. She wrote her creative prayer responses to some of the stories included in this volume. There are many other friends and teachers who have inspired me and helped me along the way. Although I cannot mention them all, I am truly indebted to their wisdom, encouragement and friendship.

I owe a debt of gratitude to my late father, Taneo Hanaoka, who told me many great Eastern stories when I was a child. He also taught me to respect his religion, Buddhism, while encouraging me to pursue my own, Christianity. His sincerity in his own spiritual journey inspired me to pursue my own path with equal sincerity.

I also wish to take this opportunity to thank my wife, Ayako, and our three wonderful children, Chris, Sayuri and Mioi. Growing up in a pastor's family is not easy, but they have all done remarkably well. I thank them all for who they are and for their loving support.

Nobuaki Hanaoka
Daly City, California

Table of Contents

Foreword

Alfred Bloom

Some years ago, I attended services in Rev. Nobuaki Hanaoka's church in Berkeley, California. There, I first heard his Asian stories from which he drew Christian insights. I was deeply impressed by his insight and broad spiritual perspective. Now he has collected those wonderful stories into a book for the benefit of readers, wherever they may be. It is my great honor to offer this introduction in the hope that others will find their spiritual horizons broadened by the stories Rev. Hanaoka recounts.

In Hawaii where I live presently, we constantly "talk story." Storytelling has been a major form of human communication and sharing wisdom and insight. The great religious traditions are all well known for the many stories or parables they employ to illustrate and clarify their religious principles. Jesus was known for his parables, such as the Prodigal Son and the Good Samaritan, which live in our religious and cultural memory. They have become symbols for various approaches to life.

In Buddhism, the parable of the burning house is well known. It describes the human condition, a world ablaze with passions. The Buddha is described as using similes and parables along with rational discourse to explain his teaching. A good story is often better than a long, complicated philosophical explanation to make a point.

i

I would illustrate the significance of this work by referring to a few of my own favorites, such as Indra's Net, which illustrates that we all are nodes in the great net of cosmic life and reality. We are gems reflecting each other and witnessing to the cosmic reality, which embraces us all. Likewise, in a story where a woman tries to evade the presence of the Buddha, we are taught that reality or the immanence of God confronts us everywhere along our path in life. It is inescapable, though we desire to evade its challenge. The story of Bodhidharma is very famous in the Buddhist tradition, giving us insight into true spirituality. It is not to be pursued for benefits and gain, but without self-serving. It reminds us, as the Bible points out, that those who worship God must do so in spirit and in truth. The poignant story of The Poppy Seeds relates a mother's despairing grief at the death of a child and her inability to accept it. It dramatically presents personal grief, and it shows how the Buddha guides her to realize the universality of death and impermanence while also expressing the preciousness of life. These are just a few of the treasures Rev. Hanaoka has garnered.

He has brought together this collection of stories to encourage and illustrate Buddhist-Christian dialogue. For several years, there has been a vigorous movement among scholars and theologians to share insights from the two major traditions and find points of commonality while recognizing significant differences. In our general society, Asian insights, and notably the practice of meditation, have become well known. Rev. Hanaoka's use of stories, drawing on his own background in Japan, greatly furthers this process. As he notes, this process is important because we live in a world of global intercultural communication and pluralism.

Consequently, a healthy spirituality for today will move from a Western either-or perspective to an Asian both-and complementarity, which permits a broader appreciation of the world's wisdom. Through the sharing of stories and wisdom, we can tap the popular mind and bring to light our universal humanity while encouraging peaceful resolution of our many modern problems.

His reference to The Ten Ox-herding Pictures used in Zen Buddhist training highlights the fact that we are engaged in a journey, or a process of transformation in insight. The stories he selected can provide the stimulus for us to ride the buffalo to our own insight.

To assist us, Rev. Hanaoka gives a general orientation to the teaching and development of Buddhism for those not so familiar with it. He also sets forth his perspective on spirituality and religion as the background for the stories he selected. I believe the readers owe Rev. Hanaoka a debt of gratitude for bringing to light these stories and making them our own, whatever our religious affiliations may be.

Alfred Bloom, Ph.D.
Professor Emeritus, The University of Hawaii
Former Dean, The Institute of Buddhist Studies,
Berkeley, California

Introduction

Spirituality and Religion in Postmodern World

Mainline churches in the postmodern societies of the West may have been declining slowly in number and influence, but, remarkably, people are still searching for more authentic and vital spirituality. Visit a local bookstore and check the religious books section, and you will find shelves of books on Eastern religions and spirituality. It means that many are looking for alternatives to their own religious traditions in search of more vital spirituality that can withstand the challenge of post-modernity, while their own churches are, by and large, failing to respond to their quest.

This book should in no way be seen as an effort to convert readers to an Eastern religion or to any form of religious syncretism; it is meant to enrich the spiritual lives of readers, regardless of their religious backgrounds. Since the religions of the West have been so deeply intertwined with the Western modes of thinking, it could perhaps use some homeopathic antidote from the Eastern spiritual heritage. The Western habit of putting everything in "either-or" terms, for instance, is not always helpful as it tends to foster polarization, while the Eastern pattern of "both-and" aims at integration toward a more harmonious whole. We must at least consider the merit of the integrative thinking of the East if we wish to leave a more peaceful world for our posterity. The traditional Eastern ideal of living in harmony with nature is another aspect of spirituality that needs to be explored if we are to look for a lifestyle that is ecologically sound and spiritually fulfilling.

We live in a truly remarkable time in history. Unprecedented progress in the speed of communication and transportation continues to accelerate globalization of the world in all aspects of life. Cohabitation of cultures and languages is almost a norm in many of our cities today. In this postmodern pluralistic society of ours, no religion, no culture, no system of moral values can automatically claim superiority over others. We can no longer speak of Christianity as "The Religion" but as one of many in the world today. By the same token, the Western civilization can no longer assume its dominance over the rest of the world. Racism, sexism, classism, sectarianism and many other "isms" are but a few of the manifestations of anachronistic efforts to cling to a past that can no longer accommodate the pluralistic and global reality of the world today.

In the face of this religious pluralism, some may feel threatened enough to reject and even demonize other belief systems without knowing what they really are. Others may be so eager to embrace anything new and fashionable that they never get to the heart of anything, thus remaining forever superficial. Most of us, however, are respectful of other beliefs while maintaining our own religious identities. That is exactly what I wish to achieve through this book.

I have been noticing in my ministry that in our churches and synagogues are many who are very religious but not necessarily spiritual. On the other hand, outside our houses of worship are many who are not religious at all yet deeply spiritual. In other words, spirituality and religiosity do not always go together. Healthy spirituality can certainly be a product of healthy religiosity, but healthy religiosity can also be a product of healthy spirituality. The relationship is reciprocal. What is urgent today is cultivating deeper and healthier spirituality.

As we seek a new way of life and spirituality that will meet the challenges of the emerging global and environmental consciousness, I believe we can engage ourselves in a meaningful and constructive dialogue with our brothers and sisters of Eastern religious traditions. In other words, we must be able to learn from what Eastern religious traditions can offer us without being defensive about our own. I wrote this book out of a conviction that the spiritual tradition of the East, such as Buddhism, has much to offer those of the Judeo-Christian tradition of the West. Religion is a cultural and institutional form of human encounters with the sacred, and as such, it is a human construct and cannot claim to be perfect in itself. Christ may have revealed the will of God perfectly, but Christianity as a religion cannot claim to be absolute or deny the possibility of a divine revelation elsewhere. God is far greater than Christianity or Judaism or any other religion.

I believe that hidden deep beneath every authentic religion is a rich reservoir of spiritual wisdom and energy. We may not share the same religiosity, but we share a common spirituality, which I believe is intrinsic to the human race. Religions are cultural, but spirituality transcends our cultural differences. I also believe that healthy and rich spirituality can be nurtured by revisiting and reclaiming the spiritual heritage of the human race. It is urgent particularly today in light of the expanding materialistic culture.

After the completion of his monumental work, *The Masks of God*,[1] Joseph Campbell wrote, "Looking back today over the twelve delightful years that I spent on the richly rewarding enterprise, I find that its main result for me has been its confirmation of a thought I have long and faithfully entertained: of the unity of the race of man, not only in its biology but also in its spiritual history, which has

---

[1] Campbell, Joseph, *The Masks of God – Primitive Mythology*, New York, 1969, The Viking Press, p. v

everywhere unfolded in the manner of a single symphony." Rudolf Otto, in the preface of his book, *Mysticism East and West,*[2] wrote, "Whether the flower of mysticism bloom in India or in China, in Persia or on the Rhine and in Erfurt, its fruit is one. Whether it clothe itself in the delicate Persian verse of a Jalaleddin Rumi or in the beautiful middle German of a Meister Eckhart; in the scholarly Sanskrit of the Indian Sankara, or in the laconic riddles of the Sino-Japanese Zen School, these forms could always be exchanged one for the other." Our shared spirituality perhaps has to do with what Carl G. Jung calls "the archetypes of the collective unconscious," written deeply into the spiritual DNA of our species.

In spite of the universality of spirituality, we cannot deny the distinctive differences that exist between the Eastern and Western religious traditions. While the Judeo-Christian tradition of the West emphasizes the absolute transcendence of God, the Eastern religious philosophies emphasize the immanence of God. In the East, divinity is believed to be immanent in nature as well as in humanity. In the Western tradition, on the other hand, the Creator and the created can never be confused. God is the absolute "Other."

The Bible tells us that we have sinned against God and, thus, alienated ourselves from the blissful union with God. When Adam and Eve ate from "the tree of the knowledge of good and evil,"[3] human beings began to live in the world of dualities — good and evil, male and female, objectivity and subjectivity, divinity and humanity, death and life, so on and so forth, and we have, hence, alienated ourselves from the primordial bliss of union with God and with each other. We have learned to discriminate one from another, and to hide our shame from God, from others, and, worst of all, from ourselves. It accounts for our essential loneliness. Because we have alienated ourselves from God,

---

[2] Otto, Rudolf, *Mysticism East and West*, New York, McMillan, 1970 p.13
[3] Genesis 3:6

and because we have been corrupted beyond repair, we must look to God's initiative for our redemption from the curse of duality through the gift of atonement (at-one-ment). That is the basic biblical scenario of our fall and redemption. In the Eastern mystical tradition, on the other hand, there was no duality from the outset. As seen in the Chinese symbol of Yin and Yang, opposites are intertwined and together form a perfect circle, the wholeness. They believe all things, including humanity and nature, are manifestations of the Self (*Atman*, *Brahma*, God). Therefore, all things are essentially sacred. The inherent harmony and sanctity of all things is believed to be everywhere, waiting to be uncovered. Therefore, "the lamp of light" is to be found within one's own self, and not outside. Buddhism has taught that one must not rely on others for salvation but find it through awakening to the Buddha-nature, which they believe is one's inmost and truest self. Eastern religionists, thus, seek to be awakened to the enlightened wisdom through meditation and mindfulness, while the Western "Abrahamic" religions (Judaism, Christianity, and Islam) seek salvation through the self-revelation of God the Creator/Redeemer and through the proclamation of the Word of God, which bestows upon the faithful the law, wisdom and grace. Each of these three religions claims its revelation/proclamation to be absolute and final.

The Western and Eastern approaches may appear op-posed to each other in this regard, but the transcendence and immanence of God are not necessarily mutually exclusive, for the transcendent God is also immanent and the immanent God is also transcendent. That is the essential paradox of divinity. The Imago Dei (God's own image in which humanity was created) in the Book of Genesis, Christ's Incarnation, and the post-Pentecost outpouring and the consequent indwelling of the Holy Spirit all point to the immanence of the transcendent God. Also in the East, the true nirvana is not believed to be accessible through our normal reason. It transcends our conventional wisdom and conscious effort. It is believed to come only by tapping intuitively into the reservoir of wisdom and the force of life that lies deep beneath our consciousness. Hence, Zen Buddhists often talk about the "gateless gate" *(mumonkan)* that keeps out those who have not had a "breakthrough" experience.

I was born into the predominantly Buddhist culture of Japan. Although I have been Christian all my life, I cannot deny the profound influence of Buddhist spirituality and lifestyle in my upbringing. The children's books I read, the stories my father and other relatives told me in my youth, and even the language I spoke were immersed in the culture and values of Buddhism. I was always aware of my cultural dual citizenship, but I was long in denial of the powerful influence of the Eastern spiritual heritage in my own spiritual formation. As I matured, however, I grew more comfortable with my Eastern heritage, and I began to consciously integrate it into my own faith journey. Some of the long-forgotten Buddhist stories that nurtured my spirituality in my youth began to resurface. I found them quite helpful in understanding some of the biblical concepts, and I began to use some of them in my sermons. The project, which I began for my own healing, has turned out to be much more than I had bargained for. It has become a rewarding and enriching journey. It has not only enriched my faith in a profound way; it has freed me to find a new way of doing theology. Readers are also invited to be open-minded and allow these stories to nurture and challenge their spiritual lives and, thus, enrich their faith journeys.

Stories, Meditation and Prayers:

Stories (parables, fables, metaphors, anecdotes, myths and legends) from the Eastern spiritual tradition are the primary focus of our reflections in this book. You may forget my comments, but you are most likely to remember the simple stories told in this volume. Some of them may remain in you and continue to speak to you for years to come. Most of the stories I am about to recount here are those I heard in my youth. Just as Jesus' unforgettable parables continue to speak to us in many different ways at different times in our lives, these stories have remained in the deep recesses of my brain all these years and have whispered to me unexpected words of wisdom, giving me insights with which to deal with difficult problems of life. I have also added some more stories I have since learned along the way.

I took the liberty of truncating some of the stories, rather than boring readers with non-essential details, and elaborating on others to make them a little more complete as stories. Some of the stories retold here originally came from ancient Pali and Sanskrit literature, and others came from various Chinese and Japanese sources, some of which were legends of unknown origins but used frequently in Eastern spiritual literature. Others were recorded anecdotes of historical personalities, but I treated them all as "stories," regardless of their antiquity or historical authenticity. I tried to locate the original sources for verification as much as possible, but I was not always successful. I recounted those stories the way I remembered them and the way they impacted me.

Unlike doctrinal formulae or confessional statements, stories leave room for a variety of interpretations, as they are a multi-faceted and multi-layered medium of communication. In my interpretations of these stories, I have certainly taken advantage of the latitude they allow, hoping to see our Eastern friends' nod of approval. It is my hope that readers will also draw inspirations and insights from these stories as they read them in the following pages.

I suggest that you stop for a few minutes after each story and meditate on it and pray. Allow the images in the story to speak to you first. When you meditate, you might want to sit comfortably, relax, and breathe deeply. In my experience, meditation is not something we achieve, but something that comes to us when we are in a right state of mind and body, to open our minds and to break into our conventional, rational thinking. Many books have been written on meditation techniques and they are readily available today; I suggest that you find one that suits your need and let it be your guide for meditation. It may not come easily at first, but I guarantee that the more you practice the easier it will become.

In prayers, we come in touch with our inmost fears and desires; we extend ourselves toward God and we respond to the Spirit's movement in our lives. In the Christian tradition, we often use scripture as a source for prayer, focusing on a scripture passage and applying it to our lives, imagining ourselves in the place of people in Bible stories, meditating on a single word or image in centering prayer. A friend of mine, Patricia Heinicke, has written some creative prayers in response to my Eastern stories. Some of them are included in the following pages. They may not look like prayers in a conventional sense, but they are examples of how our meditation can often find creative expressions in our prayer.

You may, of course, read this book from the first page to the last as you would read any other book. I hope it will be most useful as a devotional guide. After each story, you might stop awhile to meditate further as suggested above. Read the biblical passages mentioned and the author's comments and reflect on them as well. Give voice to your own response in whatever medium or whatever form. You could start a prayer journal. In addition to or instead of solitary meditation, you may also find that these stories can be powerful in a group setting where people are encouraged to share their responses, so that what began as reading simple stories can become community prayer.

The Buddha and Buddhism

Since most of the stories that appear in the following pages are Buddhist in origin, it may be helpful for the readers to read a few pages about the Buddha and Buddhism at this point. You will also find in this volume some stories from Taoist and Hindu traditions, but I hope those stories are self-explanatory.

About five hundred years before Christ, Gotama Siddhartha was born a prince of the Sakya tribe in Northern India at the foot of the Himalayas. As a privileged young man, he was able to enjoy all the pleasures of life, but he eventually became aware of the enormous suffering experienced by people everywhere. According to legend, his father's palace had four gates. When he was ready to explore the real world outside his sheltered life, he asked for his father's permission to go out of the palace on an excursion. When the permission was granted, he first exited through the East Gate on his father's chariot. Outside the gate, the young prince saw a wrinkled and feeble old man, hardly able to walk. Gotama asked his driver why the man looked so fragile. "He once was a strong and beautiful youth like you, but as years have gone by, he has become old and is no longer able to move as gracefully as he used to," replied the driver. The following day, he went out of the South Gate and saw a man on the wayside, gasping for air and groaning with pains. The driver explained to the prince that the man was ill. When he went out of the West Gate the next day, he caught the sight of a lifeless body and a procession of mourners. Gotama was shocked as he had never seen a human corpse before. The driver told the prince, "That is the final end of all living beings. Everyone dies and there is no escape from it."

Thus the sensitive young prince learned that all people suffer "aging, illness, and death." The legend does not mention the fourth gate, but "birth" was added to the list of human sufferings as perceived by young Siddhartha, for it is the beginning of all suffering.

Resolved to find a way to liberate humanity from misery and suffering, Siddhartha renounced his family and royal privileges and left the palace at the age of twenty-nine. For six long years, he went through all kinds of torturous disciplines, which nearly killed him, but he failed to find any viable solution to the quest of his soul. He then retired to a forest, sat silently under a banyan tree and began meditating. For forty-nine days, he was met with the Great Temptations. Mara, the Devil, first sent him a horde of armies. All the arrows and lances thrown at him, however, turned into flowers just before they reached him. Having realized that no external threat could penetrate Siddhartha's determined mind, Mara began to tempt him internally. He said to Gotama, "You shall become a great king who would conquer the entire world." But he remained unmoved by the temptation. The Devil then sent his three beautiful daughters to tempt him with sensuous pleasures of life, but he did not give in. After overcoming the temptations of fear, power and lust, Siddhartha came to a Great Enlightenment. He came out of the forest to the town of Sarnath, near Varnasi, and delivered his first discourse in the Deer Park. He preached and taught for forty-five years and died peacefully at the age of eighty years under a sal tree.

As Gotama himself hesitated to speak about it in the beginning, it is not possible to put the substance of his Enlightenment into words, but the following four statements might summarize the gist of it:

1) All living beings suffer
2) Nothing is permanent
3) All phenomena are in the web of cause and effect (Karma)
4) Nothing has lasting substance

Gotama's enlightenment teaches that we all suffer because we live in denial of those inescapable truths and are enslaved and controlled by things that have no substance or permanence. When you are no longer attached to them, you will be free from all things that cause suffering. A flower blooms one day and falls to the ground the next. There is nothing you can do about it, and there is no reason to be attached to its momentary attraction. In his first sermons, the Buddha formulated the foundation of his teaching in a more systematic way as "Four Noble Truths":

1) Life means suffering
2) The origin of suffering is attachment/desire
3) The cessation of suffering is attainable
4) There is a way to reach the cessation of suffering

The way to reach the cessation of suffering or Nirvana is summarized in his "Eightfold Right Path." They are as following:

1) Right understanding
2) Right resolve
3) Right speech
4) Right action
5) Right livelihood
6) Right effort
7) Right mindfulness
8) Right concentration

Karen Armstrong, in her book *Buddha*,[4] places them in three categories: 1) **Morality** (Right speech, action and livelihood), 2) **Meditation** (Right effort, mindfulness and concentration), and 3) **Wisdom** (Right understanding and resolve).

"Right," in these instances, means, first of all, having been liberated from one's selfish desires and passions for illusion, and, secondly, having compassion for all living

---

[4] Armstrong, Karen *Buddha*, Penguin Books 2001, p.82

beings. In other words, action is considered "right" when it leads both yourself and others to the peaceful state of transformed consciousness and to acts of compassion. In essence, The Eightfold Right Path encourages nonviolent thoughts and behavior, thoughtful and compassionate conduct, and a peaceful life that comes from the unification of body, heart and mind. Gotama also discerned that neither the epicurean way of self-gratification nor the ascetic practices of self-denial can lead one to the state of true freedom. Thus he advocated the Middle Way as the way of spiritual discipline.

I know I have oversimplified the early teachings of the Buddha, but to discuss it in any further detail is beyond my ability or the scope of this book. Those who wish to learn more about the early teachings of the Buddha might study some of the Pali scriptures translated and collected under the heading "The Word of the Buddha" in *A Buddhist Bible* edited by Dwight Goddard (Beacon Press, Boston, 1994). No matter how you look at it, however, the foundational teachings of the Buddha were quite simple. And as all Buddhists know, what counts is not how Gotama explained it but how one reaches the same depth and authenticity of his enlightened life. Consequently, many books have been written about the Enlightenment and how others can attain the same state of consciousness. That is why there are so many Buddhist scriptures that are considered authoritative. There are several thousand books that have been recognized as authoritative Buddhist scriptures, written over the period of two thousand years in various languages such as Sanskrit, Pali, Chinese, Tibetan, and Japanese. Some of them are highly sophisticated metaphysical discourses, others personal accounts of beliefs, and still others collections of dialogues between masters and their disciples.

That is what makes the study of Buddhism so difficult. It is so broad that a lifetime of study cannot even begin to cover the expansive body of its sacred literatures. Fortunately, however, Buddhism is not a religion of canonical books. Buddhists do not use their sutras in the way Jews, Christians, and Muslims use their sacred scriptures. Each Buddhist sect chooses from among the authoritative scriptures what it regards as helpful for its faith journey and makes that scripture its foundational document. Tolerance, magnanimity and open-mindedness are the epitome of Buddhism. Instead of wasting time and energy arguing among themselves over the validity of their interpretations, they simply practice what they believe. That appears to be the Buddhist way.

Gotama the Buddha never claimed to be a Savior, but a teacher. After his enlightenment, he reluctantly began to teach what he had found and showed his students how to live a life of freedom and compassion. Therefore, anyone who is awakened to the truth of his teaching can be a "Buddha," for the Sanskrit word simply means "enlightened one" or "awakened one." Buddhism is not about having faith in the person of Gotama the Buddha or in the efficacy of his salvific deeds, but rather about seeking an enlightenment and Nirvana that Gotama himself experienced. He taught that "The Lamp of the Light" is within you, hence, never to rely on others for salvation, even on the Buddha himself. In the Early Buddhism, therefore, a faithful devotion to the person of Gotama the Buddha was carefully discouraged. Instead, people were encouraged to seek true wisdom for themselves.

By the second century, two main branches of Buddhism emerged, namely, the Southern and Northern Transmissions or Theravada and Mahayana. Mahayana means a "Big Vehicle." It is so called because its ultimate goal is the universal salvation of all humanity, while Theravada (The Way of the Elders) tries to preserve the teachings of Gotama the Buddha, and it became a way of life for those who renounced worldly pursuits and dedicated themselves to a lifelong pursuit of the Buddha's teaching. Thus, Theravada is not a religion of laity but basically of monks. Mahayana, on the other hand, decided to honor the spirit of the Buddha's teaching by interpreting it rather liberally. With the help of the great religious thinkers, such as Nagarjuna and Asvaghosha, the Mahayana Buddhism laid a solid foundation to become a universal religion and added a large body of Sanskrit literature.

In the fourth century, the Mahayana scholarship made another significant leap when two outstanding Yogacara "Mind-Only" philosophers from Gandhara, Asanga (310-390) and his brilliant brother Vasubandhu (320-400), developed detailed analyses of the structure of mind. According to them, there are six levels of consciousness, namely the five senses and reason, but below them are two layers of unconsciousness. One is called *mana*. It is where our unconscious self-preservation mechanism resides. The other is called *alaya*. The Sanskrit word means "storehouse." The name of the mountain range "Himalaya" literally means the storehouse *(alaya)* of snow *(hima)*. In the Yogacara "Mind-Only" school terminology, *alaya* is the storehouse or the repository of karmic seeds accumulated in the unconscious level of human psyche through hundreds of thousands of years. They taught that the enlightenment had to do with altering the deepest level of the unconscious, namely *alaya*. The theory of *alaya* seems very much like the Jungian concept of the "collective unconscious" or the "archetype," [5] while *mana* seems closer to "personal unconscious." With this theory, Asanga and Vasubandhu laid a theoretical foundation for the universal spirituality that is inherent to the human race and for Zen's intuitive method of cultivating the unconscious level of human psyche.

Buddhism entered China in the mid-second century, and by the fifth century the center of Mahayana Buddhism had begun to move from India to China. There, in China, Buddhism underwent another significant transformation. The metaphysical details and mystical imaginations of Indian

[5] Campbell, Joseph, ed. *The Portable Jung*, The Viking Press, New York. 1971, p. 59-69

Buddhism were replaced with the practical orientation of the Chinese minds. The Indian metaphysics was recast into the Taoist philosophy and the Confucian morality. The doctrines and disciplines were markedly simplified. Zen and the Pure Land School are good examples of the Chinese interpretation of the Indian religion. In the sixth century, Buddhism was introduced to Japan by a Korean king, and it became popular among nobles and intellectuals. With the patronage of Prince Shotoku, it became the official religion of Japan, but it was much later in the early thirteenth century that Buddhism became a religion of the masses. Against the backdrop of the collapse of the old political system and the emergence of samurai as the new ruling class, in addition to the frequent drought, famine, wars, and epidemics, such spiritual giants as Yosai, Dogen, Honen, Shinran, and Nichiren appeared and began new movements of faith, namely Zen, Jodo (Pure Land), and Nichiren schools.

Yosai and Dogen both traveled to China and studied Zen (Ch'ang) meditation practices there. Upon their return, they began to propagate the teaching of Zen Buddhism, whose austerity and simplicity immediately appealed to the newly emerging samurai class, artists and other intellectuals. Zen temples began to spring up everywhere, along with Zen-inspired arts, such as meditation gardens, calligraphy, and tea ceremonies.

Honen and his disciple Shinran pushed the Chinese teaching of the Pure Land School to the extreme and made a radical departure from the traditional Buddhist teachings. Unlike the earlier Buddhists, who practiced mental and physical disciplines and meditation in their attempt to attain *satori*-enlightenment and nirvana, Honen and Shinran spoke for the ordinary people who could not reach *satori* by means of self-discipline and taught to rely completely on Amida Buddha's Compassion for salvation. "Simply recite *Namu Amida Butsu* to invoke the name of the compassionate Amida Buddha, and you will be reborn into the Pure Land," they taught. They called their teaching a religion of "Other

Power" to distinguish it from the traditional Buddhist teaching, which they called the religion of "Self Power." Centuries before Martin Luther and his Protestant Reformation, Honen and Shinran established the principles of "Faith Alone" and "Grace (Compassion) Alone" in their protestation against the traditional religion of Buddhism. While Zen remained popular among the samurai class, Shinran's Shin Buddhism became popular among all others, nobles and peasants alike.

Nichiren also rebelled against the traditional teachings and institutions of Buddhism. He did not believe that the religious should remain content with their personal salvation in the face of the corruption of the powerful and the misery of the poor. He boldly called for justice for the poor and the disenfranchised. Much like the Hebrew prophets who warned their people of foreign invasions, Nichiren accurately predicted the invasion attempts by the Mongols. His prophetic legacy is another aspect of Japanese Buddhism that began in the thirteenth century, and has since remained powerful to this day.

Mahayana Buddhism is practiced today primarily in China, Mongolia, Korea, Japan, Taiwan, Tibet, Nepal, Bhutan and Vietnam, while Theravada Buddhism is found predominant in Sri Lanka, Burma, Thailand, Kampuchea and Laos. If you compare Zen's austere simplicity, Shin Buddhists' faith in Amida Buddha's Vow of Compassion, and Tantric Buddhism's esoteric rituals, you may find it difficult to believe that they are one and the same religion, but they actually represent the wide spectrum of the Mahayana movement. They not only share the same roots, but also the same goal. The differences are in the methods of attaining nirvana, which is an enlightened state in which you are no longer touched by illusory desires or suffering.

The development of the early Mahayana movement coincided with that of the Early Christian Church. When the Early Church theologians were struggling to reinterpret the teachings of Jesus and his apostles, as seen in the theological diversity of the four Gospels and the Gnostic literature, the Mahayanists were also trying to interpret the teachings of the Buddha in their own contexts. When Paul and John were writing their theologies in Asia Minor, slightly to their East, in Gandhara and Central Asia, Mahayanists were writing theirs. Just as the eschatological expectation of the End-Time and the physical resurrection of Jesus were recast in the existential spirituality of the Fourth Gospel, the Mahayanists were also reinterpreting the Buddha's teachings to meet the new spiritual needs in their own existential context. Though there were significant differences in their approaches, the parallelism between the development of the Early Church theologies and the Mahayana movement is undeniable, and, as you will see in the following pages, their theological themes and spiritual sentiments were remarkably akin to each other.

As they shared the early trajectories of existential struggles in search of deeper and more authentic spirituality, thus contributing to the development of these two great religious traditions, Buddhists and Christians can come together again in dialogue in search of new spirituality that will withstand the challenge of the twenty-first century without compromising the integrity of either tradition.

Chapter One:

The Journey

*The sun and the moon have been on their journey for eons;
so have the years that come and go. Life is a journey; and
the journey is home to the boatman whose life drifts away on
the waters and to the horseman who grows old leading his
horse by the mouth. Many died on the journey, but there was
an irresistible urge within me to set out, as if possessed by
the seduction of the wind of patchy clouds or by a lure of the
god of journey.....*

(Preface to "Narrow Road to the Deep North," Matsuo Basho)

1

On the Back of a Buffalo

$\mathcal{L}$ong ago in China lived a learned man who spent most of his waking hours reading scholarly books and contemplating the lofty wisdom of ancient sages. One day, he chanced upon a book that discussed the virtues of a remarkable animal called "buffalo."[6] The animal is big and powerful, yet gentle and kind, proud and independent, yet humble and always ready to render assistance to anyone with a heavy burden. Whether you are rich or poor, young or old, noble or lowly, it makes no difference to the animal. Furthermore, the female of the species produces milk even to nurse human babies.

Deeply touched by what he had learned about the virtuous animal, the man set out on a journey in search of a buffalo. He traveled up and down the river, beyond the hills and far into the vast continent of China, never realizing, however, that the very animal he was riding was none other than the animal called buffalo.

ॐॐॐॐॐॐॐ

Zen Master Po-Chang (720-814 CE), while instructing a young monk Tai-an in the way of Zen, said to him, "Searching for the Buddha-nature is like riding an ox in search of an ox." You may spend your lifetime searching for

---

[6] "Buffalo" here refers to Asian buffalo, the large ox-like bovid animal. The so-called "buffalo" often associated with the American Wild West actually is "bison."

it, but you will never find it until you realize that you are on the back of what you are in search of.

ॐॐॐॐॐॐॐ

The same truth applies to our search for God: We may seek God's grace, but we are already in its warm embrace, whether we deserve it or not. Likewise, the God we seek to know and understand is the One who dwells in us and enables our seeking. God above, therefore, cannot be known apart from God within. After all, God is, in the words of St. Augustine, "more intimate than I am to myself *(intimior intimo meo)*."[7]

In the first chapter of the Gospel according to John, the author describes his theology of incarnation in these words:

"The Word became flesh and dwelt among us;
we have seen his glory,
the glory as of God's only heir[8], full of grace and truth."

John is saying here that the transcendent God has become flesh in the life of Jesus of Nazareth and, hence, become immanent in the humanity of Jesus. Later in the fourteenth chapter of the same Gospel, Jesus, in preparation for his own impending departure, promises his disciples that the Holy Spirit, as God's indwelling presence, will be given to them when he is no longer with them "in flesh." In other words, God's Spirit dwells within us now and guides us through our journey of life, teaching us all things necessary for the journey.[9]

---

[7] Ingram, Paul O. *Wrestling with the Ox: A theology of Religious Experience* (New York, The Continuum Publishing Co., 1997, p. 110)
[8] "God's only son" according to NRSV.
[9] Luke 14:26

Thus, we detect in John's Gospel a two-step process of God's self-identification with or self-immanence in us — from God the Transcendent to Jesus the Incarnate, and from Jesus the Incarnate to the Spirit's indwelling presence in us. John's was not the lone voice in the New Testament speaking of the mystery of God's immanence, as Paul also spoke often of "Christ (living) in me."[10] A typical Western theology, however, has emphasized the absolute Other-ness of the transcendent God, but often failed to mention that the same God is immanent in the humble and mundane reality of life on earth.

❦❦❦❦❦❦❦

Following Po-Chang's ox metaphor, his disciple Tai-an asked him further, "Master, what does one do after finding the ox?" "One goes home on the back of it," replied Po-Chang. In a typically cryptic way of Zen speech, "going home on the back of an ox" means making reentry into life as one who has made peace with the ox (i.e., one's inmost self, the Buddha-nature, or even "God within") and integrated it into one's own life.

At around the end of the ninth century, inspired probably by Po-Chang's ox metaphor, Zen artists created what you might call a pictorial guide to Zen practice. They simply called it *The Ten Ox-herding Pictures*, as it consisted of a series of ten pictures. It has been widely used as an aid to Zen training, but it also suggests stages of our spiritual journey in search of a buffalo. The first picture shows a child looking for an ox. The following pictures show the boy finding the traces of the ox, then finding, catching and taming the ox; he then goes home happily on his back. In the seventh picture, the ox is no longer in the boy's mind. The eighth picture shows only an empty circle, signifying that the

---

[10] ex. Galatians 2:20

child now lives as if neither he nor the ox mattered. The journey has now made a complete circle, after which the child enters the village offering bliss and peace to all, as all dualities have now ceased and all is in perfect unity and harmony.

The illustrations found in the chapter pages of this book are from a contemporary rendition of *The Ten Oxherding Pictures* by a marvelous wood-block print artist, Tomikichiro Tokuriki.[11]

❧❧❧❧❧❧❧

The Buddha-nature (*Buddhata* in Sanskrit) is believed to be one's inmost and truest self, which Buddhists believe is an immanent form of the transcendent. Therefore, a journey in search of the divine is actually a journey in search of one's true self as well.

We are now embarking upon a journey, and ours is a journey in search of the God who transcends us but dwells in us as well. It will be an exciting process of finding ourselves in God and finding God in ourselves, in the world and in nature. In so doing, we may be able to cross the ocean of dualities, overcome the split in humanity and the rift in the world and reach the yonder shore of peace, synthesis and wholeness.

This journey, however, is not just an individualistic pursuit of inner peace alone, for out of the Great Calm of the Spirit within must come compassion for all and passion for justice and peace in the world. Thus, ours is an inward-outward journey. The journey is particularly pertinent today, as races are pitted against each other, the natural

---

[11] In this book, the pictures do not appear in the originally intended order, but in Appendix I at the end of the book, all ten pictures are printed in the original order.

5

environment is being destroyed at an unprecedented speed, and our planet, crowded with unprecedented 6.6 billion people, is still plagued by loneliness and alienation.

On the back of a buffalo, let us now set out on a journey in search of a buffalo for a more authentic discernment and awareness of the One who nurtures, heals, sustains, and moves us from within to a more peaceful, just, humane and compassionate world.

The Raft

*O*nce upon a time, there was a young merchant. He traveled far and wide to conduct business. One day, on his way to another country, he came upon a river; but the bridge he expected to see there had been washed away in the storm during the night, and the river was still swelling. "I cannot swim across the river," he said to himself. "It is too dangerous. On the other hand, if I waited for the water to recede, it would take days, which I cannot spare."

At his wit's end, he was gazing aimlessly upon the swift water. Suddenly, he saw something totally unexpected. From upstream came a raft floating down the river. "This indeed is a gift from heaven!" he exclaimed. Quickly he pulled it toward the shore and stepped on it. When he had safely reached the other shore, he said to himself, "What a wondrous gift this is! This indeed is a heavenly blessing that makes the impossible possible. I shall cherish it as my most treasured possession as long as I live."

Early in the morning the following day, he resumed his journey with that heavy raft on his back. As he looked up, he saw the imposing figure of the mountain he now had to scale, towering high above the mist of the canyon and glowing in the morning sun.

"Like unto the raft, all truths indeed must be abandoned, let alone untruths!" warns the Vajracchedika Prajnaparamita (Diamond) Sutra.[12]

---

[12] The full text of the Diamond Sutra in English is now available on the Internet at www.diamondsutra.us and at some other Buddhist websites.

The sutra refers to the raft only as a metaphoric image, but the image of the raft is so striking that it has since been developed into a parable and used often in Buddhist literature. Like many of Jesus' parables, this is basically an observation of what we humans do, often unaware of its foolishness. There is a sense of humor in it, too. Buddhist interpreters relate this to the way some people cling to the doctrines of their own religious traditions. Buddhists have doctrines also, but they seem to be remarkably free from them. They consider the doctrines only as a tool with which to communicate some of their basic teachings; the doctrines themselves are never mistaken for eternal truth.

One of the most important principles of Zen Buddhism is that of *"Fu Ryu Mon Ji"* or "No Reliance on Letters." The letters and words might help us in the beginning, but if we continue to rely on them, we might miss the most important truth that cannot be expressed in words. An ancient Chinese philosopher, Lao Tzu, said it beautifully at the beginning of his *Tao Te Ching*:

> *"The tao that can be told*
> *is not the eternal Tao.*
> *The name that can be named*
> *is not the eternal Name.*
> *What is eternally real is unnamed."*[13]

While the raft may be helpful in crossing the river, it is a burden in scaling the high peaks. Life's journey consists of "letting go" of something old and "grabbing" something new. Unless you let go of what is in your grasp, you cannot grab anything else. But when you let go, your hands are free to grab on to something new. That seems to be an important lesson in the art of life. Words may be a necessary guide

---

[13] Mitchell, Stephen, trans. *Tao Te Chin* (Harper & Row, New York, 1988) p.1

until you reach a certain place in your journey, after which they can be an impediment for the journey ahead. Some of us are totally devoted to our raft. But when we have crossed the river, we need to let go of it and let the Spirit take over. The Spirit will send us other unexpected helpers along the way. We all want to hang on to something familiar and tangible, such as the old doctrines of the church, the letters of the scriptures, and their literal interpretations. I suppose that is human nature, but the reward of letting go of the raft and letting the Spirit take over is perfect freedom.

The Dragon Ship

By the mid-seventh century, the center of Buddhist studies had moved from India to China, and many students from all parts of Asia flocked around large temples and monasteries of China where prominent scholars gave lectures daily. Among those foreign students was a handsome young monk from Korea named Uisang (625-707 CE). All Buddhist monks, those days, even great scholars among them, would walk to a nearby town or village every day to receive alms. The honorable tradition of mendicant priesthood, which originated with Gotama himself, was not only a good training tool with which to teach monks humility, but also gave people a chance to earn their karmic merit through almsgiving. Hence, monks, clad in black robes, holding only a walking stick and an iron bowl, and chanting a sutra on street corners, was becoming a familiar sight in China. Whenever a voice of sutra chanting was heard outside, people would rush out of their homes for the privilege of placing a fistful of grains or vegetables into the monk's bowl.

Uisang also went out to town every day to receive alms. One day, when he was holding his bowl and chanting a sutra as he did every day, a beautiful young lady, Shanmiao, came out of her house to give him a handful of rice. She was a daughter of a certain nobleman in the country. When she saw the young monk, she immediately fell in love with him. From that moment, all that mattered to her was Uisang. She thought about him constantly, and she couldn't even eat or sleep well. She found herself waiting for him every day, and as soon as she heard his chanting, she would rush out of the house to give him alms. A few weeks passed, and Shanmiao could no longer contain her feelings. She mustered up all her courage and asked him to come into the courtyard of her house, and there she confessed her love to him. Unfortunately, however, he had to tell her that he could not respond to her love because of his vow. She knew priests could not marry and that she had no choice but to accept it. In time, her romantic passion for him appeared to have been sublimated into a sincere devotion to assisting the young monk.

When she learned that Uisang had completed his studies in China and was going home to Silla, Korea, she bought him an expensive priestly robe and a new bowl as parting gifts. When she came to see him off, however, the ship had already left the harbor; it was only a dot on the horizon. Determined to see him again, Shanmiao threw herself into the sea. The moment her delicate body hit the water, she was transformed into a mighty dragon. She swam to Uisang's ship at an amazing speed and carried it on her back. A powerful typhoon was in the area, but Shanmiao, now a mighty dragon, protected the ship and carried it safely to the shore of Korea, where Uisang later founded the Kegon (Flower Garland) School of Buddhism.

ৡৡৡৡৡৡৡ

In the archive of Kozanji Temple of Kyoto is a famous set of thirteenth-century scrolls called *Kegon-shu Soshi Eden* (Illustrated Stories of the Founder of the Kegon School). It is registered and protected as a national treasure of Japan. In it is a picture of a ship crossing the treacherous sea as seen in the next page. The ship may be pitching and rolling in the roaring sea and the ferocious winds, yet those listening to the priest aboard appear to be remarkably calm and undisturbed, for underneath is a mighty dragon protecting and carrying the ship on its back.

11

(Kegon-shu Soshi Eden, National Treasure, 13th century, Kozanji Temple, Kyoto, Japan. Used with permission from Kozanji Temple.)

The ship in the picture symbolizes the subjective aspect of life's journey. We feel happiness and peace when circumstances are favorable, but the feeling can quickly turn into that of insecurity, anxiety and uncertainty when we are met by storms of life. The ship, however, is being carried on the back of a dragon. In the East, dragons symbolize the positive force of life. In this particular case, it is a symbol of the unknown and indefinable force that sustains life and moves us forward in our journey to the yonder shore of wholeness and synthesis. Therefore, no matter how turbulent the sea and how ferocious the wind, the ship sails on safely because of the dragon that is mightier than the destructive forces of wind and sea. Yes, the rift may be deep and the crossing hard, but we must trust in the unknown force that sustains us and carries us to the far shore of wholeness and synthesis.

Reflecting on the picture, James Ashbrook[14] says that the most fundamental longing of our heart is to reach wholeness, but to reach it we must cross the turbulent sea, which is to live the split that defines the reality of life. Ashbrook writes, "To become a part of the whole, we must participate in the part that we are. To overcome the rupture in our humanity, we must <u>be</u> the split that we have become, then we will be the whole that we are not yet, yet are to be."

[14] James Ashbrook, *Humanitas - Human Becoming & Being Human,* Nashville: Abingdon Press, 1973, p. 19

To live as a human being is inevitably to experience a split between the reality and the ideal, the actual and the potential, the conscious and the unconscious, etc.

The rift between races is a common experience in our society. It has inflicted many deep wounds and indescribably painful memories in the hearts and minds of many and has weakened us all. The source of the problem seems to lie in our sense of insecurity. An honest acknowledgment of our own insecurity can awaken in us healthy recognition of our need for others, but it can also make us feel threatened by elements unfamiliar to us. We must admit that we are all guilty of prejudices, as we feel intimidated by those who look and act differently and often react to them in unhealthy manners. Racism is certainly a split that needs to be crossed in our society and in our hearts, for no race is complete in itself until all races can live in harmony and mutual respect. Likewise, sexism and homophobia give us a sense of incompleteness and anxiety. Adam's shout of joy, "At last, this is the bone of my bones, flesh of my flesh" (Genesis 2:23), reflects humanity's primordial longing for overcoming the split and attaining new synthesis.

৵৵৵৵৵৵৵

In biblical language, this unknown force is called the Holy Spirit. Trust in the power of the invisible Spirit, which is mightier than any other forces we might encounter in our journey of life. Trust it completely, and you will have peace even in the midst of a ferocious storm of life.

In the fourth chapter of the Gospel according to Mark, we find a fascinating story of Jesus calming the sea. Jesus first says to the disciples, "Let us go across to the other side." By those words, he is calling us to overcome the split in life and to strive to attain a new synthesis. When they were crossing the sea, a storm arose suddenly and the boat was about to sink. The disciples were frightened, but Jesus was sleeping peacefully in the stern. They woke him and said, "Teacher, do you not care that we are perishing?" Jesus got up and commanded the storm, "Peace! Be still!" As soon as he had spoken those words, the wind ceased and the sea was calm again. In this story, Jesus was at peace because he represented the force of life, the dragon as it were, in which is peace and calm even in the midst of the storm. Jesus made the disciples aware of the presence of the force by commanding the sea, "Peace! Be still!"

691691691691691691691

Join Patricia in her prayer in response to our story of the dragon ship:

The storm hurls its word of destruction and we cower,
throwing back our own words---
weak curses, threats, promises---
eaten scornfully by the wind.

Thus we sit on your back, Dragon God.
Few of us sense your rooted strength beneath us,
moving within the storm, solid and graceful.
We cannot release ourselves to you,
for you are great and veiled,
your voice hidden inside the storm's.

Most of us do not recognize you:
We imagine you long drowned.
Your presence breaking through
seems the storm's peculiar cruelty,
or it slips away, an unattended Mystery.

Some of us ride you like a bronco,
mistaking the storm's fury for yours.
Your unfettered wake seems test or temptation;
we try to break you with frightened righteousness,
with anxious logic to wear you down.

We are frail, O God,
small to stand against the onslaughts
of lightning and wave,
loneliness and disease,
sorrow and exhaustion.
Out of the depths we cry to you,
Witness the disquiet of our souls.

Look on us with your kind Eye.
Teach us to hear your Voice within the storm,
to trust your way beside our fear.

Make our hearts bold to listen to your Spirit,
to feel your Body beneath us,
to lean into the Wind.

— Patricia Heinicke, Jr.

The Mischievous Monkey

𝒯here is an epic adventure novel called *The Journey to the West*, [15] popular for centuries among children throughout Asia. It is about a well-known Chinese Buddhist priest, Hsüan-tsang (602-664), who journeyed to India to obtain a new set of Mahayana scriptures. Some unusual travel companions joined him along the way. One of them was a mischievous monkey, who possessed certain supernatural powers. He had a respectable name, Wukong, but he was basically a "rowdy misfit."

One day, Wukong the monkey boasted to the Buddha that he was able to summon a patch of cloud and travel on it hundreds of miles in an instant, suggesting that he would easily be able to get out of the Buddha's reach. The Buddha said, "Try it." So the monkey called on a patch of cloud and jumped on it. He then traveled on it as fast and as far as he could. When he saw colossal pillars reaching high into the heavens, he knew he had reached the end of the universe. He produced a giant paintbrush and wrote on one of the pillars, "I have reached the end of the universe, far out of the reach of the Buddha." Upon his return, he proudly reported to the Buddha, "I have just been to the end of the universe, far out of your reach." The Buddha smiled and showed his palm to the monkey and said, "Read what is written on my finger right here." It read, "I have reached the end of the universe,

---

[15] *Hsi-yu Chi* in Chinese. The one-hundred chapter novel is considered one of the four great treasures of Chinese literature. It was originally published in China in the late sixteenth century during the Ming dynasty.

far out of the reach of the Buddha." He had never left the palm of the Buddha.

ক্তক্তক্তক্তক্তক্তক্ত

No matter where you are, you are always on the palm of God's hand. You may lose yourself in the maze of this confusing and confused world. You may, at times, feel as though you are far out of God's reach, but you are never really lost, because you are always on the palm of God's hand, and that is our home.

Homecoming is always very special. Home is a place you can always go back to. It is your base. As a child, whenever I came home from school or a friend's house, I would always holler at the door, "Mom, I'm home." Invariably, she would holler back to me, "Okaerinasai!" It meant "Welcome back. I am glad you are home safely." I always liked my mother's voice saying that magic word. It instantly made me feel welcome, loved and safe. However, no matter where we are, we are always home because we all live on the palm of God's hand and we are all members of one family. No matter what the circumstances of your family may be, no matter where you are in relation to your biological family, you are always home, God's home.

Our society is becoming less and less homogeneous, and some of us may be feeling threatened by its diversity. But remember, God's world is always our home. Whatever economic status you may have, whatever educational level you may have attained, whatever race or cultural group you belong to, it doesn't matter. We have been told that Black or White or Brown or Yellow, 99.9% of our genes are identical, regardless of race. We all belong together, and we are all home. Life indeed is a journey, but the journey IS our home. No matter how far we have traveled in the journey of life, and no matter how far we have yet to go, we are still on the palm of God's hand. We are home.

We find the same sentiment expressed most beautifully in Psalm 139, in which many of us have found comfort and solace.

O Lord, you have searched me and known me.
You know when I sit and when I rise,
you discern my thoughts from far away.
You search out my path and my lying down,
and are acquainted with all my ways.
Even before a word is on my tongue,
O Lord, you know it completely.
You hem me in, before and behind,
and lay your hand upon me.
Such knowledge is too wonderful for me,
It is so high that I cannot attain it.
Where can I go from your spirit?
where can I flee from your presence?
If I ascend to heaven, you are there.
if I make my bed in Sheol, you are there.
If I take the wings of the morning,
and settle at the farthest limits of the sea,
Even there your hand shall lead me,
and your right hand shall hold me fast.

The Flying Turtle

$\mathcal{O}$n an old pond somewhere in the subcontinent of India lived a proud little turtle. Turtles are not generally known for a talkative disposition, but this one was. In fact, the residents of the pond and the surrounding forest called him Gabby the Turtle behind his back. Since we don't know his real name, let us call him Jonathan Livingston for the time being. His excessive loquacity was generally attributed to the obvious gap between his limited physical mobility and the disproportionately active imaginations of his mind. Jonathan could swim freely in the water, but, once out of the water, the weight of his shell made his walking quite awkward and difficult. There was no question that his shell had served him well as protective gear because it kept him alive for so many years, but for an intelligent, freethinking turtle like Jonathan, the limited mobility was quite frustrating.

On that fateful morning, as usual, his motor mouth was the only thing heard around the otherwise serene old pond. A couple of swans descended gracefully upon the waters for a little respite on their way to the Russian tundra. Jonathan was the first to greet them, as you might expect.

"Good morning, my friends. My name is Jonathan Livingston. On behalf of all the residents here, I welcome you to the pond. If you are resting here on your annual journey, please feel free to take as much time as you wish."

"Yes, thank you. We will be on our way soon," they responded.

"It must be nice to travel and see the world," said the turtle enviously.

"Yes, we enjoy it. Because we fly at high altitude over all kinds of terrain, we get to see many different types of scenery."

"That's wonderful. Look at me. I am always stuck here in this muddy pond, and nothing interesting ever happens around here."

"But it is nice and quiet here. It seems that you have enough food, too."

"It's too quiet here, and I am tired of eating the same old food all the time. I would like to be able to get out of here and see the world, but I can only fantasize about it. I wish I could fly like you."

"That would be difficult because you have no wings. Let me see…"

One of the swans was in deep thought for a minute or so and then said to him, "See this stick, Jonathan? I will grab this end of the stick and my sister can grab the other end, and you hang on to it at the middle with your teeth. You have powerful jaws, do you not? That way we can carry you in the air."

"That's a brilliant idea. Let's try it."

"Okay, I am ready if you are."

Their plan worked beautifully, and they were soon in the air, flying. Jonathan was enjoying the ride immensely as he had never seen the wide expanse of the terrain from above. Below him were dark forests, blue mountains, meandering shiny rivers, neatly kept rice paddies and villages. Everything was breathtakingly beautiful.

When they were flying above a village, children looked up and saw this strange sight in the sky – a turtle flying with swans. They laughed, jeered, and shouted, "Hey, turtle. Don't you know who you are? You are a dumb turtle and you are supposed to be stuck in muddy waters. You look silly up there."

Hearing that, Jonathan was terribly offended. He thought to himself, "They are witnessing a truly historic moment. They should be inspired by what they are seeing instead of making fun of me." After a while, he could no longer resist the urge to shout back at them. The moment he opened his mouth to shout, however, he began to fall from the sky four hundred feet to the ground.

ॐॐॐॐॐॐॐ

The original versions of the story were told both in the Pali and Sanskrit Canons. A relief depicting the story has been found in cave sanctuaries in Java as well as in India. It even made its way to *Aesop's Fables* in Europe and to *Konjaku Monogatari* (Once-Upon-a-Time Stories) in Japan. In the Pali Canon of Theravada Buddhism, the turtle fell onto a palace garden belonging to a king who was known for his hasty and careless verbal remarks to everyone. The king took a lesson from this unfortunate incident and learned to think twice before opening his mouth. In the early twelfth century collection of tales, *Konjaku Monogatari*, the story concludes, "Beware; excessive talk can thus destroy your life."

ॐॐॐॐॐॐॐ

The story has been universally interpreted as a warning against excessive and careless talking. We all know it is the tongue that often gets us into trouble and hurts others. Apostle James seems to have been painfully aware of it himself and wrote thus in his letter: "So also the tongue is a small member, yet it boasts of great exploits…no one can tame the tongue—a restless evil, full of deadly poison" (James 3:5 & 8).

There is, however, another lesson to be learned from the story. It is that of accepting what is inevitable in life gracefully. Of course, we all dream of being where we are

21

not and becoming what we are not. That's how progress is made. We cannot blame our turtle for dreaming about flying away from his little world. We would have liked him to succeed in his venture. We empathize with him, as we see in him the same quest that drove Jonathan Livingston Seagull to his repeated, dangerous attempts at flying ever higher and faster. There are times in our journey when we must defy accepted standards and conventional knowledge and push the limit even at the risk of life.

On the other hand, there is a haunting question: Did it ever occur to our turtle that his being what he was and where he was may have been God's great gift? O Jonathan, your limited mobility could have given you a rare opportunity to observe, really observe the amazing beauty of the pond and the mystery of the forest, to listen to the music of the wind, and to appreciate the intricate harmony of nature around you. In fact, the mystery of the entire universe was right there before your eyes. Your life there was a privilege, Jonathan, and not a curse. The most sublime experience of the deepest mystery of life was unfolding right before your eyes and you did not see it.

Journey to India

$\mathcal{D}$espite all the fictitious characters and incredible adventures recorded in *The Journey to the West,* its principal character was modeled after a true historical figure, the venerated Buddhist priest called Hsüan-tsang. He was a philosopher, linguist, and adventurer as well. In the year 629 CE, at the age of twenty-nine, he began his journey to India to obtain some new Mahayana scriptures and to study the philosophy of Asanga and Vasubandhu. He actually traveled through the vast desert of Central China, the bandit-infested Western borders and the frozen peaks of the Tienshan Mountains before entering India, where he studied under the greatest scholars of his time for a few years. Upon returning to China, he began translating the Sanskrit texts he obtained in India into Chinese. By the time he finished the work, he had translated 1,338 volumes of Sanskrit texts into elegant Chinese. Among them, his translation of Hridaya Sutra, which consists only of 266 Chinese characters, is truly a gem in the annals of spiritual literature and is still recited daily by Buddhists throughout Asia. It took him eighteen years to bring the Sanskrit texts to China and seventeen years to translate them.

When an English archeological team, led by Hungarian-born Marc Aurel Stein, unearthed a huge collection of ancient Buddhist texts from the sand-covered caves of Dun Huang, near the Western borders of China, in 1906, they found among them an old manuscript of the Hridaya Sutra. In its preface is the following story:

Soon after Hsüan-tsang began his journey, he met a very sick Indian monk in an abandoned temple. Hsüan-tsang stayed with him and nursed him back to health. Grateful for his kindness, the Indian monk taught him a short Sanskrit sutra called Hridaya (Heart) and told him to recite it whenever he encountered danger. Hsüan-tsang committed it to memory and recited it throughout his journey. When he finally reached India, the same monk met him there again and told him that he was actually Bodhisattva Avalokitesvara disguised as a sick monk and that it was the power of the sutra that had brought Hsüan-tsang safely to India.

In the middle part of the Sutra are two pairs of lines that are really the heart of the so-called Prajna-Paramita philosophy:

Form is no other than emptiness.
Emptiness is no other than form.
Form is exactly emptiness,
Emptiness is exactly form.

In the first and the third lines, the text teaches that all phenomena that can be observed with our senses have no substance. We may be attracted and attached to them, or we may be repulsed and offended by them, but they are merely passing and illusory. The beauty of an attractive person, for instance, may catch your eyes and even steal your heart, but her or his skeleton, which is the only lasting thing in the person, has no beauty at all. Likewise, our achievement, status, wealth, pride, power, knowledge, and even what we might consider a matter of life and death are all empty.

The second and the fourth lines are not just a rhetorical reinforcement of the first and the third, but provide a new twist. Emptiness is not a negative thing, according to this philosophy. Emptiness and fullness are one and the same. The Sanskrit word for emptiness, *sunya*, is also used to indicate "zero" in Indian mathematics. Actually, the concept of zero was invented in India. Zero is neither negative nor positive, but the center of all numbers. *Sunya* (zero/emptiness), though indefinable, defines all things; though uncontainable, contains all things. In other words, the emptiness that is in all is that which embraces all. When we discern the emptiness of all things, we can appreciate them all as manifestations of that which embraces all things. We are now free from them all, but can appreciate them and even love them all. The paradox of this Great Emptiness reminds us of the holy Tetragrammaton, YHWH (I-AM), the most sacred name of God, who transcends all things but embraces all things as well. "Emptiness" may be just another name for God.

It sounds corny: To love something, you must become free from it. To love someone truly, you must be ready to let go of that person. In the words of Jesus, "What is born of the flesh is flesh, and what is born of the Spirit is spirit…You must be born from above" (John 3:6-7). Jesus is not rejecting the flesh. After all, he is the Word made flesh. Yet, in order to accept the flesh (and all other tangible and mundane objects), one must renounce it first and receive it anew. I believe that is the meaning of the new creation and the resurrection life. To free our spirits, we must begin the journey from attachment to detachment, then from detachment to a free, new engagement in life. That seems to be the heart *(hridaya)* of the Buddhist teaching, and perhaps also of the Christian spirituality.

ॐॐॐॐॐॐॐ

My father would sit in front of his portable altar at home and chant this sutra every morning. I never joined him in chanting it, but because I heard it coming from his room every day, I learned it by heart. Even with my limited classical Chinese, I could follow most of it, especially if I had the text in front of me, but at the end of the sutra were a couple of lines of Chinese characters that did not make sense at all. Yet, if you heard it chanted slowly, it had a strangely calming effect. It went like this:

"Gate, Gate, para-gate, parasaw gate, bodhi svaha…"

I later learned that this part of the sutra was not a translation, but a phonetic transliteration of the Sanskrit text. No wonder it did not make sense in Chinese. I also learned later that it meant: "Hail to those who have gone beyond, gone beyond to the other shore. The blessed enlightenment! So be it!" It was a beautiful benediction, but why did Hsüan-tsang not translate this last beautiful verse of the sutra? Perhaps he did not consider it important for everyone to know its precise meaning. Perhaps he just wanted people to pronounce those mysteriously soothing sounds as a mantra at the end of the sutra. I believe Hsüan-tsang understood the healing power of mantra incantation. Not everything has to be comprehended intellectually, but just knowing the sound of its truth may be sufficient.

"Gate, Gate, para-gate, parasaw gate, bodhi svaha..."

Chapter Two:

Roads to Peace

Then justice will dwell in the wilderness,
and righteousness abide in the fruitful field.
And the effect of righteousness will be peace,
and the result of righteousness, quietness and trust for
ever. My people will abide in a peaceful habitation,
in secure dwellings, and in quiet resting places.

— Isaiah 32:16-18

Indra's Net

$\mathcal{F}$ar, far above in heaven, there is a realm where Indra, the king of gods, lives. There hangs a canopy of magnificent net made of fine silk, undoubtedly the work of many extraordinary craftsmen. It is so vast that it stretches out indefinitely in all directions, and a glittering jewel is set on each node of the net. Since the net is infinite in size, the jewels are also infinite in number. Like the glistening stars you see in the sky above on dark nights, the jewels are brilliant and innumerable. The magnificence of Indra's jeweled net is matched only by that of his power and glory. If you pick one of those jewels for inspection and look closely at it, you will discover that in its polished surface are reflected all the other jewels in the net, infinite in number. Not only that, each of the jewels reflected on the surface of this one jewel also reflects all the other jewels, so that the process of reflection is also infinite.

ð≈ð≈ð≈ð≈ð≈ð≈ð≈

I read "Indra's Net" first in a children's book of the same title by Kenji Miyazawa. I was not aware of it then, but it was originally written more than a thousand years ago in one of the supplements to the ancient text of Avatamsaka (Kegon/Hua-yen/Flower Garland) Sutra, and it has since been studied by the devotees of the Kegon School of Buddhism. It was noticed recently by Western scholars and has been endorsed by philosophers and physicists alike. Its recent popularity in the West is not so much because the metaphor accurately represents the core Mahayana

28

philosophy, which it does, but because it serves well as a conceptual model of the emerging pluralistic world and also of the universe as contemporary physicists see it.

Indra's Net teaches that all things are in the web of interconnectedness and inter-causality. Nothing exists or happens in isolation. Everything reflects everything else. At each intersection of time and space (at each node of horizontal and vertical threads of Indra's Net) is an individual entity, which is connected to all others through the web, and each entity reflects all other individual entities indefinitely, just as two mirrors facing each other reflect each other's image indefinitely. In other words, each and every entity is a reflection and embodiment of all others.

This Mahayanist concept of "interconnectedness" or "mutual identity" obviously contradicts the Western ideal of the autonomous self and self-reliance, which has shaped much of the mainstream modern Western thinking. In the Cartesian modern science, for instance, the cosmos is simply a collection of numerous unrelated and independent entities. Therefore, in the West, each individual person has been seen as a distinctly independent being. Likewise, everything that happens is a pure accident, unrelated to what has happened elsewhere. Those who attempt to connect the dots without observable evidence are looked upon as unscientific and superstitious. Hence, religious persons who see God's hand in various events often collide with those immersed in the Cartesian assumptions of modern science.

On the other hand, Mahayanists have always assumed that every entity is interrelated to every other entity. Individuals are not seen as independent as they are interdependent. In addition, there is no such thing as an accident; everything is part of the infinitely extending and delicate causal relationship in which even the slightest change in one affects all others. Hence, some have called Indra's Net a model of "cosmic ecology." When we begin to live that

29

interconnectedness, they believe, we can act more compassionately toward each other.

Christianity, Judaism, Islam, and Buddhism are all bright jewels in Indra's Net; each sheds its distinct light, yet each reflects all others. The purer, the brighter, and the more beautiful each jewel is, the more purely, brightly and beautifully it reflects others. Exclusiveness, absolutism and ignorance are no longer acceptable in this pluralistic, global society. In the face of mass starvation, ethnic cleansing, genocide, the AIDS epidemic, poverty and nuclear proliferation, those of us who stand on the rich spiritual legacy of our religious traditions have no time to waste in fights against each other, each claiming superiority and demonizing others. We must learn to respect and work with each other, for we have so much to do today to protect life, its dignity and its environment everywhere in the world.

こ*こ*こ*こ*こ*こ*こ*

We have entered the age of a new frontier, cyberspace, where theoretically all of us are now connected through the Internet. Some have suggested that Indra's Net is a perfect metaphor for what the Internet can and ought to be. Like Indra's Net, the Internet is infinite in size, and the jewels in it are infinite in number. Each website can be linked to all others, and all are interdependent. We have an infinite amount of information at our disposal. It is our hope that our humanity has matured enough and evolved enough to use the power we now possess wisely to further our respect for each other and to protect life and dignity of all in the world. With the power we now have, we have no more excuses.

A Celestial Nymph

$\mathcal{V}$imalakirti Sutra [16] is one of the more enjoyable texts among the early Mahayana literature. Vimalakirti, after whom the sutra was named, was a merchant by trade, but the profoundness of his wisdom eclipsed that of monks and scholars. The idea that a layperson surpasses monks and priests in the knowledge and wisdom of eternal truth and that he finally finds his equal in the likes of Shariputra and Manjushri, who were the Buddha's wisest disciples, makes this literature definitely Mahayana.

In the sixth chapter of the sutra is an interesting scene in which a celestial nymph makes her appearance. She eavesdrops on a fascinating dialogue unfolding inside Vimalakirti's house — a dialogue between Vimalakirti and Manjushri. Manjushri asks, "In what must one live if one wishes to remain in the greatness of the Buddha?" Vimalakirti replies, "To remain in the greatness of the Buddha, one must live in the equality of all beings." As the dialogue continued, the maiden was so intrigued by what she was hearing that she could no longer contain herself. She descended into their midst and showered all who were there with fragrant petals of celestial flowers. When they began to shake them off, the celestial maiden asked Shariputra, "Why are you shaking them off?" "Because it is improper for us, who have renounced the impermanent world, to adorn

---

[16.] A modern Japanese translation of *Vimalakirti Sutra* is found in *Daijo Butten (Collection of Mahayana Sutras)* (Chuo-Kōron-Sha, Tokyo, 1969), pages 83 to 194. Since the Sanskrit version exists only in fragments, the translation was made from a Tibetan version.

ourselves in the vanity of flowers," Shariputra replied. "Listen, Wise One," she insisted, "these flowers cannot undo your renunciation. Attachments and discriminations come from within, not without. Look, the flowers are stuck on those who have not overcome their attachment to senses, but not on those who are truly liberated."

Impressed by the nymph's wisdom, Shariputra asked, "O heavenly maiden, do you not wish to become a man? With your supernatural power of magic, you could certainly become like one of us." The maiden did not appreciate the insinuation that men were superior to women. She said, "I have been exploring what it means to be a woman for many years, but I have not found the answer yet. Suppose a magician can change a man into a woman, do you think she would want to be turned back to a man again?" "But a magician's tricks are illusion," said Shariputra. "Precisely," she replied without a moment's hesitation, "all appearances are illusion! Neither male nor female actually exists!"

Then, with her supernatural power, the celestial maiden turned Shariputra into a woman and herself into a man. In a sarcastic tone of voice, she asked, "O Wise One, do you really want to become a man again?" Shariputra did not know what to say because he was not able to comprehend what had happened to him. The nymph said, "All beings are neither male nor female, as Gotama the Buddha has said. A female person is not just a female. A male person is not just a male." At that point, the nymph changed their appearances back to what they were, and asked, "Where has your femaleness gone, Wise One?" Shariputra said, "When you changed my appearance, I remained the same person inside. Yet, I was a woman." "That is precisely the point," said the heavenly maiden, "You are who you are, no matter what gender you happen to be."

This intriguing tale could be a story straight out of the modern feminist movement, though it was actually written almost two thousand years ago. This particular tale displays a remarkably liberated mind, but there are many other sutras that discriminate against women and even demonize them. Do women really distract men's spirituality like demons? "Don't try to shake them off," the nymph says. It won't work. If you are free inside, the flowers would not stick to you anyway; but if you are un-free, they will be stuck, no matter how hard you try to brush them off.

The world consists of men and women. You cannot avoid or demonize the other half of the population just because you are vulnerable to their attraction. "Don't blame us; the problem is yours." That's what the heavenly maiden was saying in this story. We must be more careful and more caring when it comes to gender issues. It is a wonderful gift from God. To degrade the opposite sex is to degrade your own, because male and female are but two aspects of the humanity we all share. We need each other to be complete. To reach the yonder shore of wholeness and peace, we must learn to cross the ocean together.

Harp of Burma

$\mathcal{T}$oward the end of World War II, in the chaos and insanity of the Pacific Asian theater of the War, there was a Japanese outfit known as the "Singing Company." They were facing stiff opposition from the British troops trying to retake Burma (Myanmar) from the Japanese occupation. Battles were fierce and casualties mounting on both sides. Everyone was weary of fighting, killing and getting killed. To keep a shred of humanity in the inhumanity of war, the commanding officer, Captain Inoue, who had majored in music in college, taught his troops to sing songs of various countries in the world. In the company, Corporal Mizushima was by far the most talented. He taught himself to play his handmade Burmese harp and often accompanied their singing. He also played his own compositions to calm the nerves of the weary soldiers. They all loved his gentle spirit and his exquisite music.

Running out of ammunition and also of men, the captain decided to move his platoon, now reduced to a handful of injured men, across the border to Thailand, deemed friendlier to Japanese. When they arrived at a small, isolated village in the jungle near the border, the villagers gave them permission to stay there one night. The scouts, however, found that they were completely surrounded by the British and there was no way out. They knew that they were trapped and they were all going to die in a final, desperate battle that night. As they anticipated an all-out attack by the British troops in a short time, Corporal Mizushima began to play his harp and the others joined him in singing:

Mid pleasure and palaces though we may roam,

be it ever so humble, there's no place like home.
A charm from the skies seems to hallow us there,
which seek thro' the world, is ne'er met with else-
where. Home, sweet home, there's no place like home,
there's no place like home.

As they sang, they noticed that many more voices were coming from the dark jungle around the village. Soon, all the soldiers, British and Japanese alike, came out of hiding, and, with tears in their eyes, all sang together *Home, Sweet Home* in beautiful harmony.

That night, they were informed by the British officer that Japan had surrendered to the Allied Forces three days ago. They were also told that there was another Japanese unit in the mountain still fighting. He asked if someone would volunteer to go into the mountain and tell them that the war was over. Corporal Mizushima volunteered, and the rest of them were sent to the prisoner-of-war camp in Mudon. A few days later, they learned that the Japanese soldiers in the mountain were all killed, including Corporal Mizushima with them.

Three months later, a slim Burmese Buddhist monk with a harp was seen near the camp. Those who saw him said he looked like Corporal Mizushima. A few months later, aboard a ship bound home for Japan, the soldiers sang the song. Suddenly, out of nowhere, the Burmese monk appeared on the shore and began to play his harp to their song. Some of the soldiers recognized him and began to shout from the ship, "Mizushima, let's go home." "Mizushima, come home with us." The monk responded only with a sad look and he disappeared.

When the ship had left the harbor, the commander read to his soldiers the letter from Corporal Mizushima. "Dear Captain, I am reporting to you my activities since I left you on a mission. I did go to the mountain to try to persuade our fellow Japanese soldiers to stop fighting, but they would not accept Japan's defeat and wanted to keep fighting until the last soldier. I failed in my mission. While I was still there, the British began the bombardment on us. Apparently I was the only one who survived the bombing. I was unconscious for a few days. When I regained consciousness, I was being cared for by some villagers. When I realized that they might be a tribe of head hunters, I got scared and ran. I ran toward Mudon, where you were detained. On the way to Mudon, I disguised myself as a Buddhist monk for safety. The corpses of dead soldiers were everywhere, in the jungle, in the fields and on the riverbanks. I started to bury them, one by one. But there were so many of them. I wanted to go home with you, but I cannot leave Burma until I have buried all the fallen soldiers who fought in this senseless war and chant a sutra for their peaceful repose. Please understand."

ෙ෯෯෯෯෯෯

Harp of Burma was written originally as a children's novel by Michio Takeyama (1903-1984), professor of German literature at the Tokyo University. It was later made into a critically acclaimed motion picture twice by Kon Ichikawa. This touching story shows how the madness of warfare violates the sacred bond that binds human hearts together. Though it is hard to believe, human beings are not only capable of waging such a bloody and senseless war, but also of singing together in harmony across the enemy lines. Both stupidity and nobility are part of human nature.

This may not exactly be called a Buddhist story, except that it comes from the long line of traditional Japanese Buddhist accounts of war, starting with the twelfth-century classic, *The Tale of the Heike,*[17] which describes the fall of the powerful warrior clan Heike:

---

[17] An epic story about the fall of the once thriving warrior clan Heike (Taira). The story was written in a ballad form and sung usually by wandering blind minstrels.

*"The temple bell of Jeta Grove[18] echoes the
impermanence of all things.
The color of sala soju[19] flowers speaks of the law that
the prosperous must eventually decline;
and, like a dream on a spring night,
the proud shall not endure;
and the mighty shall fall at last.
Like dust before the wind,
they all perish without exception,
and the arrogance of the victors shall never last...."*

There is no winner in war. The only thing left after
the bloodshed is a profound sense of tragedy. How long does
it take for us to understand the absurdity of war? With our
nuclear capability today, it is even more absurd than ever
before. Yet, we still fight. The Cold War is over, only to be
followed by the "holy" wars in the Middle East, the ethnic
cleansing in Bosnia and now in Somalia, and the war for a
"regime change" in Iraq, only to be followed by the endless
series of sectarian violence and the further radicalization of
terrorism. How long, O Lord, how long will it take for all in
the world to refuse to fight but learn to sing together in
harmony?

---

[18] Jeta Grove is where Gotama Buddha had his first temple. Most of his
early sermons were preached there.
[19] Sala Soju (Double-blossomed sal tree) has large, brilliant flowers.
They bloom in the morning, but by the evening they drop to the ground.
Hence, the sal flower has become a symbol of life's impermanence.

Simplicity as a Way of Life

A few years after he attained Buddhahood, Siddhartha visited his family at the invitation of his aging father, the king. The reunion at the palace was very sweet, and it delighted his father immensely. The next day, however, Gotama took his begging bowl and went out to town to receive alms. The king was greatly disturbed when he heard that his son was going from door to door begging for food. The king went forth in haste and met his son. He said, "Why do you have to disgrace me like this? You know I can provide for all your needs." The Buddha said, "Father, this is the custom of my family." "How can that be? Ours has always been a royal family. None of your ancestors begged for food like you. It is a sheer disgrace," remonstrated the father. "Great king, I am talking about my Buddha family. All the Enlightened Ones before me lived on alms. To us, poverty is not a disgrace. Humility is our way of life."

Later, when Gotama was in the kingdom of Magada, he went out to the farm owned by a Brahman, who was distributing food to his laborers. When he saw the Buddha standing there with a bowl in his hand, the Brahman said, "We eat because we have tilled the soil, planted the seeds, and gathered the harvest. Our food is the fruit of our labor. What have you done to deserve yours?" "Brahman, I also till, plant, and harvest," the Buddha responded. "But I don't see your plough or ploughshare, cow or yoke. How can you say you till, plant, and harvest also?" asked the Brahman. The Buddha answered, "The seed I plant is faith. Meditation is our rain. Our plough is wisdom, and our plough-stick, penitence; our yoke is contemplation, and our ploughshare the depth of our contemplation. We keep ourselves from evil; we speak kindly to others and eat modestly. We remove weeds with the wisdom of truth, and enjoy a blissful rest when our labor is done. A disciplined spiritual life, which is our cow, will carry us home to the peace and bliss of Nirvana." The Brahman saw the import of the Buddha's labor and became his follower.

కికికికికికి

As seen in the above stories, the Buddhist tradition of mendicant priesthood began with Gotama himself. The Sanskrit word *bhikkhu*, whose typical English translation is "monk," literally means "one who begs for food." Thus the begging bowl held in the hand of a Buddhist monk is a symbol of poverty and humble dependence on the surplus of others for sustenance.

Buddhist priests' ceremonial stole, called *kesa* in Japanese (from Sanskrit *kesaya*), is made of *jo* (strips) of discarded fabrics. A *kesa* of seven *jo*, for instance, is a stole made of seven different strips of materials others have disposed of. Hence, the begging bowl and *kesa*, in the mendicant tradition, have become the symbols of the spiritual values that have shaped a counter-culture in the midst of the society that idolizes the rich and powerful.

The excavation of Mohenjo Daro has revealed that the great civilization that flourished from 2500 to 1500 BCE on the plains of the Indus River was actually based on excessive environmental exploitation. The material comfort the urban population enjoyed required an excessive exploitation of the natural environment, and their sewage system steadily washed away the nutrients of the soil until it was no longer able to produce what it took to sustain the population. The once glorious civilization disappeared, leaving only the ruins of its infrastructure, not because of a foreign invasion or a natural catastrophe, but because of the gradual destruction of its environment by overuse and misuse.[20] A civilization that thrives on excessive exploitation of the environment and wasteful consumerism dies of the very thing that made it prosperous in the first place.

The Book of Genesis states explicitly that God gave humans dominion over all of creation. Hence, the Judeo-Christian tradition has often been blamed for the exploitation of the natural environment. However, in reality, many other civilizations, including that of Mohenjo Daro, have contributed to environmental disasters throughout history. Also, it was not only Eastern philosophers who taught us to live in harmony with nature, but some Christian teachers as well, such as St. Francis of Assisi (1182?-1226). Francis required all the members of his order to honor the vow of poverty, and he taught them to respect all living things and inanimate objects as if they were their own brothers and sisters.

In light of the dwindling fossil fuels, the thinning ozone layer, and the disappearing rainforests, we must understand that this fragile nature cannot support the affluent lifestyles we have become accustomed to much longer. Poverty, as a voluntary way of life, has again become a viable option today. Ascetic rigor alone cannot effect lasting lifestyle changes on a large scale, however. To live in simplicity, one must be able to find the spiritual wealth that is far more satisfying than material comfort. In other words, we must find the "buffalo" that carries us home to the bliss of peace and compassion.

---

[20] Dubos, René, *A God Within*, Scribners, New York, 1972, p. 154

Chapter Three:

Divine Mystery

見三
牛

There the angel of the Lord appeared to him in a flame of fire out of a bush; he looked, and the bush was blazing, yet it was not consumed. Then Moses said, "I must turn aside and look at this great sight, and see why the bush is not burned up." When the Lord saw that he had turned aside to see, God called to him out of the bush, "Moses, Moses!" And he said, "Here I am." Then he said, "Come no closer! Remove the sandals from your feet, for the place on which you are standing is holy ground."

— Exodus 3:1-6

Hidden in Plain View

At nearly eighty years of age, Gotama's once strong body had become considerably weaker. Although he was not ready to retire from his ministry, he was forced to put off his plan of traveling farther to Kosala temporarily and settle in a small town near Vesali of Licchavi to recuperate from his recent illness. He was often seen meditating alone in a garden nearby. Sometimes, however, when the sun was gentle early in the morning, he would take a long, leisurely walk in the countryside.

Now, this is a story everyone used to know. In the town where Gotama the Buddha lived, there was a wealthy woman who, for some reason, did not like him at all. Perhaps she had some misunderstanding about him earlier, or there was simply a bad chemistry between the two. Whatever the reason, she could not stand even the sight of the saintly man. It was difficult to avoid anyone in a small town like hers, but she usually made it her business to know exactly where he was at any given time so that she could adjust her activities to stay clear of him. She was doing well with that, but one day, when the woman was traveling on a lonely road, she saw the Buddha walking toward her from the opposite direction. Between them was no crossroad or byroad or even a large tree to hide behind. Caught by surprise, she quickly turned her face away from him. She turned to the right, but the Buddha was right before her eyes. She turned to the left, but he was there as well. She looked up, and he was seen there. She looked down, he was still there. No matter which way she turned, the Buddha was seen right before her eyes. She finally covered her eyes with her hands, but through the little opening between her fingers, the Buddha was still smiling to her.

Inevitably, a few minutes later, they met on the road. They finally talked, and she became one of the staunchest supporters of the Buddha and his ministry. When truth confronts us, there is no way of denying it or avoiding it; we just have to face it.

ॐॐॐॐॐॐॐ

This story brings back the memories of my father because it was from him that I first heard the story. "This is a story everyone used to know," he would begin his stories. I was quite young then, eight or nine, but I remember vividly all the humorous gestures with which he told the story. After hearing it a few times, I learned to turn my head to the right and to the left, up and down, with my father, and watched for his eyes to appear slowly between his slightly parted fingers at the end. He was ordinarily a very dignified and stoic man and I had never seen him look so silly. That, perhaps, was why the memory of this comical story was registered in my memory so vividly.

What I heard as a funny little children's story over fifty-five years ago was actually a story about the inescapability of *Buddhata* (Buddha-nature) or the divine mystery and beauty in all things. Buddhists believe that no matter how much one may try to deny it or avoid it, *Buddhata* is hidden everywhere in plain view — in all beings. Thus, all persons, however evil, are sacred.

ॐॐॐॐॐॐॐ

The Eastern pattern of thought emphasizes the immanence of God in all things. Therefore, to them, all things in nature, including humanity, are forms of the formless manifestations of the divine. On the other hand, the Western theology is focused on the absolute transcendence of God. God is the Wholly Other. In other words, the separation of divinity and humanity is essential to the Western system, although hints of God's immanence are found throughout the Bible. The first chapter of the Book of Genesis, for instance, tells us that God created the first man in God's own image and likeness. Hence, God's image (Imago Dei) is believed to be inherent in humanity. Also, in the second chapter, when God had formed Adam from the dust *(adamah)* of the earth, God breathed into Adam's nostrils God's own breath/spirit *(ruah)*, and Adam became "a living being" (Hebrew: *nephesh hayah*). Regardless of our ancestry or class, educational or economic level, we all share the same humble origin — dust — yet we all have been made sacred by God's own breath/spirit that dwells within. In other words, God's indwelling spirit, *ruah,* makes all human beings sacred. (Dr. Alfred Bloom has brought to my attention that in v. 19 of the same chapter, the exact same Hebrew phrase, *nephesh hayah*, is used in reference to animals in creation, suggesting that it is not humans alone that can claim God's *ruah*/spirit, but animals as well. They are also made sacred with the same breath of God. What an insight! It further suggests that God's immanence is not just in human beings, but in animals as well.)

The original state of innocence, however, did not last very long, according to the biblical account. When Adam and Eve had eaten from the tree of the knowledge of good and evil, they began to live in the world of dualities — good and evil, life and death, male and female, subjectivity and objectivity, etc. When they began to live in the world of dualities, the primordial state of unity and harmony was lost. The Imago Dei was thus distorted by humanity's self-alienation from the integrated and integrating whole, God. The story of the self-alienation from the blissful primordial unity was quickly followed by that of Cain's murder of his own brother, Abel. The rest of our history has been one incident after another of the separation and strife between God and humanity, between one human being and another. This alienation (rift, rupture, split) is the true face of the "original sin." Many of us seek reconciliation and unity, but in the real world, the force of polarity and rupture is indeed powerful. That is why, in Christian theology, the redemption of humanity is believed to come from the death of Christ on the cross, which was the divine act of atonement (at-one-ment) and reconciliation.

Eastern philosophy, on the other hand, has always assumed and affirmed the immanence of the divine in all things, and as I have already mentioned, the divine within is called Buddha-nature. It affirms us, ennobles us, and enables us to accept and love ourselves and others. Because it does not discriminate, it is a great equalizer as well. That is why the Buddha himself tried to abolish the caste system that had kept much of India divided since the invasion of the Vedic Aryans centuries earlier. Yet, in his *sangha* (community of monks), race and class were considered completely irrelevant, as he believed and taught that the sacred that was deep within transcended all social, racial, ethnic and individual distinctions, making all persons equally sacred.

In Buddhist and Hindu Asia, people greet each other by stopping to put their palms together in a posture of worship whenever their paths cross. They recognize and honor *Buddhata* in each other first. To them, each and every meeting is an encounter with the divine.

In the Christian tradition, many beautiful liturgies have been developed with which to worship the grandeur of the transcendent God, but not a single liturgy has been written with which to recognize and celebrate the immanent God who is present in each other. I believe it would help us see more clearly the presence of the holy in each other and in the world and overcome our prejudices and hate that have plagued our world so long.

A Butterfly's Dream

Chuang Tzu was a fascinating philosopher. Like his predecessor Lao Tzu, Chuang Tzu was a proponent of the Way of Nature, known as "Tao" in Chinese. He was born in southern China in the mid-fourth century BCE and lived as one of the independent freethinkers during the most chaotic and turbulent period in China's history. Chuang Tzu and Lao Tzu have both been named founders of the Taoist religion, but neither of them actually had anything to do with the founding of the religion. They were Taoist philosophers, but Taoism as religion came much later.

Of the two, Lao Tzu is, perhaps, better known to the West, as his *Tao Te Ching* has been widely translated into modern languages and he has become almost an icon of non-dualistic, ecological philosophy. While Lao Tzu's *Tao Te Ching* consists entirely of short, captivating verses, the book *Chuang Tzu* is more verbose and complex and is known for abundant use of metaphors and examples taken from ordinary life to illustrate his extraordinary thoughts. Here is an example:

I, Chuang Chou,[21] had a dream one day. In that dream, I was a butterfly flying about happily without a care in the world. The butterfly in the dream had no idea that it was Chuang Chou. But when I awoke, I was suddenly aware that I was Chuang Chou. Then I began to wonder whether I had just dreamt that I was a butterfly or the butterfly is now dreaming that it is Chuang Chou. Between Chuang Chou and

---

[21] Chuang Tzu's real name. "Tzu" at the end of a personal name is an honorific term often used to indicate a great teacher.

the butterfly there must be some distinction. [But I cannot tell which is more real between the butterfly in Chuang Chou's dream and Chuang Chou in the butterfly's dream.] This is what I call transitory formation.[22]

❧ ❧ ❧ ❧ ❧ ❧ ❧

Here, Chuang Tzu questions the basic assumptions of our cognitive ability by raising a fundamental epistemological question: what is reality? How do you know it is real? Can you really tell something is real and not just a projection of your mind? Chuang Tzu would say it is perception that makes what is real real. In short, "reality is perception." If so, there is no such thing as absolute objectivity or an absolute distinction between reality and illusion. Besides, what is real at one moment may not be real at the next. Likewise, what is real to one may not be real to another.

In Chapter 18, Chuang Tzu relates an encounter with a skull:

When I was traveling through the Province of Chu, I saw a dry skull of a dead man lying on the roadside. I wondered how he might have died and how his body was left there without proper burial. I took pity on the dead man, but the skull took offense at that and retorted, "How do you know it's bad to be dead? Would you like to hear how much fun I am having now? I don't have to answer to any king or general. While I was alive I never felt as free as I am now."

Again, he writes, "Mo-Sho and Li-Ki have been universally known as the most attractive women in history, but beauty is a relative concept. No matter how attractive they may look to us, fish would be frightened of their appearance and dive deep into the water. Little birds would fly away in

---

[22] *Chuang Tzu* Saying #27, Chapter 2—Equality of All Things

fear as high as they can; and a flock of deer would scatter trembling away" (Saying #20, Chapter 2).

Beauty and ugliness are relative, and so are good and evil. All dual and discriminating thoughts must be considered relative before the Way that affirms all and embraces all, according to Chuang Tzu. There is nothing absolute in this world. Subjectivity and objectivity are relative. There is no clear distinction between the observer and the observed, either. In reality, the observer is part of the observed and the observed is part of the observer.

While he questions our cognitive faculty, he affirms the Way (Tao) as the only transcendent and absolute reality that embraces all things. Tao is that which causes all things to be. It is like our Creator God, but Tao is not personal, but "natural." Chuang Tzu shuns all human machinations, volition and artificiality. He believes that Nature has a way of making all things right without us plotting what we desire or what we believe to be right.

Life and death are also relative, according to Chuang Tzu. He has this story to tell:

Tzu Lai became seriously ill and was dying. While his family was gathered around his bed crying, Tzu Li came in to see the dying friend. Leaning against the door, Tzu Li said cynically, "The great Creator? What will he make of you now? Will he make you into a rat's liver or a bug's elbow?" Tzu-Lai replied, "It is wrong to blame the Creator for my dying state. Nature gave me my body so I may live in it, my life so I may work, my old age so I may enjoy, and my death so I may rest in peace. If you think life is good, then death must be as good. . . . The universe is like a great furnace and the Creator is a master ironsmith. What becomes of me is entirely up to him. If he is going to give me death, I will rest peacefully. If he wants to give me life, I will wake up again."

කිකිකිකිකිකිකි

The Tao of Nature transcends life and death. Life and death are the two sides of the transcendent Tao and there is no essential difference between them. Therefore, if you truly understood the Way, then you can say, "It is good to live according to the Way of Nature, and it is also good to die according to the Way of Nature."

As I was translating the last part of the above story, I was thinking of the eighteenth chapter of the Book of Jeremiah, in which God is likened to a potter making a vessel on the wheel. The similarity between Chuang Tzu's image of an ironsmith and Jeremiah's potter is undeniable, but what is interesting is the fact that Chuang Tzu identifies the Tao of Nature as the Creator. The Chinese word for nature, "Zi-ran," literally means "that which makes it so" or "that which unfolds by itself." In other words, nature is what unfolds by itself without human interferences. In the biblical tradition, nature is God's creation, but in Chinese thinking, Nature is the Creator. The Chinese word for nature itself implies that, and the Taoist philosophers simply expanded on it.[23]

Chuang Tzu is basically saying to us: Trust in the goodness of Nature and face whatever comes your way with peace and grace. Don't panic, stay calm. Leave all to the Way of Nature, the Eternal Tao, and all will be fine. You will be able to enjoy all things that Nature provides so generously.

Chuang Tzu's faithful reliance on the Eternal Tao of Nature somehow reminds me of the Pure Land School's faith

---

[23] The English word "nature" comes from the Latin "natura," and it was a translation of the Greek *physis* (φύσις), which originally meant the innate way in which plants and animals grow on their own accord. Therefore, the original meaning of the word "nature" is essentially the same as that of Chinese "*Zi-ran*" or Japanese "Shizen."

in Amida Buddha's Compassion and even Paul's faith in God's grace. Lao Tzu's influence in the development of Zen has often been discussed, but it seems to me that Chuang Tzu's influence on the Pure Land School must also be recognized. When Buddhism was later introduced to China, the people understood the Indian religion in terms of the Chinese concepts and sensibility as articulated by Lao Tzu and Chuang Tzu centuries earlier.

China at the time of Chuang Tzu was not exactly a peaceful and prosperous land. Invasions, betrayals, assassinations, pillaging, ugliness and struggles were all too frequent, and they were all caused by human ambitions for power and dominance. Given the circumstances, it is understandable that Chuang Tzu was skeptical of human capacity for harmony and reason. Instead of seeking a just society in the midst of endless wars, he sought comfort in the harmony and reasonableness of nature/Nature.

I do agree with Chuang Tzu that our humanity is often selfish, destructive, and capable of ugly thoughts and cruel deeds, but I also know that human beings can be loving and compassionate beyond imagination. Like Chuang Tzu, I find myself truly in awe of nature's beauty and generosity and am often disappointed at humanity's inability to be good, just and reasonable, but isn't humanity part of nature also? If so, humanity's mental faculty must also be part of nature. Chuang Tzu saw Nature as God, but I feel the spirit of the compassionate God working in nature as well as in humanity. God is probably hoping that we humans might learn God's wisdom and generosity from the way of nature.

Elephant God

*O*ne day, a Hindu guru taught his student that every being is essentially identical to the power that supports the entire universe, namely Brahma, and Brahma is none other than Atman, or the Self. The student was so moved by it that he wandered out into the road in a state of profound rapture. Then came a huge elephant in his direction, but the student was still in his blissful state of contemplation. The driver on the elephant's head shouted, "Get out of the way, you idiot! Can't you see the elephant coming?" Having heard that, the student thought to himself, "I am Atman, the Self. So is the elephant, for all things are Atman, the God. Should God be afraid of God? Should God get out of the way of God?" The student remained in a deep meditation, undistracted by the driver's repeated warnings, until the moment of truth came, when the elephant wrapped its trunk around the student and hurled him aside. He flew off the road and onto a heap of dirt. Physically bruised, spiritually stunned, and intellectually confused, he returned to his guru. "You told me that I was God, master." "Yes, you are God," said the guru. "You told me all things are God." "Yes, all things are God," echoed the guru. "That means the elephant was also God, doesn't it?" the student inquired. "Yes, that elephant was God, but why didn't you listen to the voice of God, shouting from the elephant's head, to get out of the way?"

ॐॐॐॐॐॐॐ

This definitely is a Hindu story, because it is about the unity of the *Brahma* (Creator God) and *Atman* (Self).

That was precisely the point where the Buddha departed from the traditional Indian philosophy, as he taught that neither the *Brahma* nor the *Atman* had substance; they were both illusion. But it could be a good illustration of the Taoist and Buddhist logic that truth often presents itself as two opposing realities — Yin and Yang. I remember my father's favorite scroll, which he often hung prominently in the alcove of our Tokyo home. On it was written in Chinese a Zen adage: *"Sho Ji Ichi Nyo"* (Life and Death, One Reality). Life and death may appear to be two opposing extremes, but they are but two faces of one and the same reality. They seem to negate each other, yet they are inseparable. There is no death without life and no life without death.

When I was old enough to study philosophy, I came across Dr. Kitaro Nishida's essay entitled "Absolutely Contradictory Self-Identification."[24] According to him, the processes of identification and differentiation are an integral part of reality's ongoing process of self-unfolding. The concrete world is "a process of mutual-identification of the mutually contradictory." Nishida was seeking a way to integrate subject and object, universality and particularity, in order to overcome the world of dualities. He called the process of integration the "self-identification of the absolutely contradictory." I remember having a hard time following his logic, but it is true that while God the Perfect One and humanity, whose nature it is to be imperfect, are absolute contradictions to each other, God and humanity eternally seek to be one with each other. He saw the real world as dynamic tension of opposites seeking to be integrated, but, unlike Hegelian dialectics, his philosophy does not seek synthesis as a higher point of resolution of

---

[24] Nishida, Kitaro, "Zettai Mujun Teki Jiko Doitsu," *Nishida Kitaro Zenshu-Complete Works of Kitaro Nishida*, (Iwanami, Tokyo, Vol. 9, 1965) p. 147 The expression is hard to translate, but the German translation of the essay is entitled *Die Einheit der Gegensätz* (The Unity of the Contradiction).

opposites. Instead, he says, "contradiction is in itself integration." That, I believe, is the meaning of the phrase "absolutely contradictory self-identification."

To achieve peace, whether personal or social, one must simply see oneself in the ongoing universal process of the "self-identification of the absolute contradiction." Peace will not come until we begin to see our differences as different manifestations of the same reality in the process of its self-unfolding.

A Courtesan Bodhisattva

*A*s soon as he graduated from seminary and was ordained into priesthood in France, his order sent him to Japan and assigned him to a small working class parish in Tokyo. His name was Father Gounod. He majored in the Japanese language and literature in college, and that was probably a reason for this assignment. He was a gifted linguist, and two years of additional studies after his arrival in Japan gave him an excellent command of the language. He had no trouble understanding the language, but he failed to understand the complaints coming from the lay leaders of his parish. In his analysis, they were too serious about too many things. They insisted that they must meet every week after church until things were smoothed out in the church. "Obviously, they have nothing better to do on Sunday after church," Father Gounod concluded. He knew that the Japanese Catholics tended to be a bit more serious than their French counterparts, but their seriousness was beyond comprehension. They were concerned about every little thing their priest did in the church and even outside the church. They complained that he looked like a communist when he invited a leader of the local union to talk about the latest labor dispute in the factory where many of his parishioners worked. They also complained that his sermons were too short, yes, too short. He had never imagined that anybody would complain about that, but short sermons were not scholarly or dignified enough, according to them. After a while, however, things began to go reasonably well, although he was still finding the somber mood of the church a bit suffocating.

One Sunday, a very attractive woman, elegantly dressed in a kimono and seated on the pew, caught his eyes during the Mass. She was so beautiful and her mannerism so graceful that she looked radiant, like a bright star in the dark sky of his congregants. Her name was Satoko, which he memorized on her first visit to the church. When he invited her to the Catechism class, she surprised him by her immediate response, "Yes, I would love to. I need to learn more about Christianity." The lay leaders of the church, on the other hand, were quite upset about this. "Father, this is not a church for a geisha like her," one of them said to him. Father Gounod didn't know she was geisha, but didn't understand why it mattered. All he knew was that her presence in the church was a breath of fresh air, a very special gift indeed. Fortunately, the matter did not have to be resolved right away.

During his Catechism class, the Father asked her,

"Satoko, what brought you to the church?"

"It's my karma," she replied.

"Karma?" he inquired.

"It was the day of the first anniversary of my mother's passing. I wanted a place to sit quietly and pray for her soul, and I happened to see the steeple of your church. That's how it happened. What else than karma could it be?" said Satoko.

Father Gounod was amused that she did not hesitate to use the Buddhist word to explain her visit to the Christian church. He might have said "Divine Providence," but the phrase would not have occurred to Satoko. He simply smiled and said, "I see." Even though it did not make sense to him, he knew it made perfect sense to her. It appeared that to her, everything was a result of her karma. She was a geisha because of her karma. She found the church because of her karma. She was preparing for baptism because of her karma. Father Gounod knew that Satoko's amazing capacity to accept everything inevitable with such grace and gratitude had to do with her understanding of karma, and he decided not to argue with her about it.

A few months later, Satoko stopped Father Gounod after church and said, "Father, I am dancing in this recital. Will you honor us by your presence?" "Of course, Satoko, I wouldn't miss it for the world," replied the Father. Pleased to hear him say so, Satoko handed him a scented envelope with a ticket to her dance recital in it.

On the day of the recital, Father Gounod arrived at the theater early enough to read the program. He learned that the number Satoko was going to dance was entitled *Shigure Saigyo* (Saigyo the Priest in Autumn Rain). It is based on a true story of a famous encounter of a celebrated twelfth century poet-priest, Saigyo, with a courtesan by the name of Tae.

When Saigyo was traveling near the village of Eguchi, where there was an infamous brothel, it began to rain. He knew it was a place of ill repute, but he needed a place to stay for the night — it was raining and he was too tired to travel any farther. So he came to the brothel and asked for accommodations for the night. A courtesan by the name of Tae answered the door. Seeing that the man was a priest, she refused. Saigyo quickly wrote a verse on a piece of paper and handed it to her:

> *Though difficult it may be*
> *to renounce the temporal world entirely,*
> *How difficult could it be*
> *to offer me a temporal room?*

She then wrote in return:

> *Since you have*
> *renounced the fleeting world,*
> *I did not wish to tempt you back*
> *to the attraction of the temporal world.*

In other words, she refused him lodging because she did not want the priest to be tempted to the fleeting attraction of the temporal world. After exchanging those verses, the courtesan invited the priest in and they talked all night. For the sake of historical accuracy, I might add that the courtesan Tae left the brothel soon after she met Saigyo and later became a nun. She eventually founded a temple nearby and dedicated it to all the women of the brothel at Eguchi. Today, more than eight hundred years later, the brothel is gone, but the temple still stands at the original site and the names of famous courtesans and not-so-famous harlots are still seen on the tombstones of the temple cemetery.

Now back to Satoko's recital: In the middle of the dance, the courtesan suddenly turns into a Bodhisattva and reveals that she was actually Bodhisattva Samantabhadra (Fugen Bosatsu) in disguise. Her quick and dramatic transformation from a courtesan to a Bodhisattva can be a big choreographic challenge, but it is the central part of the dance as it tries to remind us of the Mahayana teaching that all persons have the Buddha-nature, even harlots. Father Gounod was profoundly touched by the elegance of the dance and the beauty of the story, and he renewed his resolve to baptize Satoko no matter what the lay leaders of the church might say. Like Mahayanists, Father Gounod knew that God is in everything and everyone God has created, sanctifying and ennobling all beings, even a geisha like Satoko.

ঔঔঔঔঔঔঔ

This story comes from Sawako Ariyoshi's award winning collection of short stories, *Eguchi no Sato*.[25] As a Japanese Catholic, she was trying to find within herself a place where the predominant religion of her culture, Bud-

---

[25] Ariyoshi, Sawako, *Eguchi no Sato*, Chuo-Kōron-sha, Tokyo, 1979

dhism, and her own faith, Catholicism, could meet and shake hands with each other. To her, it was the presence of the sacred in every person, whether it is called the Buddha-nature or the Imago Dei. That is also the place where humanity and divinity can embrace each other and the East and the West can coexist in peace.

The peace of the world depends on our ability to see the divine in each other, regardless of the person's culture, religion, ideology, ethnicity, or occupation. "Whatever you did to the least of my brothers and sisters, you did to me (Matthew 25:40)," said Jesus. I wish we could all treat each other with respect and love, because even the most unlikely person you see today may be a Bodhisattva or Christ in disguise.

The Rich Father and the Poor Son

*O*nce upon a time in India lived a man who loved his son very much. The father noticed that the son had been a bit rebellious lately, but he thought it was a phase that would pass quickly. Then, suddenly, the son ran away from home, apparently enticed by his friends into an illusion of carefree independence. To tell the truth, he wanted something a little more exciting in life, too. After leaving his peaceful home, the prodigal son explored life a little and enjoyed its excitement, but the money he had taken from his father's house did not last very long. As soon as his money was gone, so were his friends. Destitute and alone, he wandered from one strange town to the next, begging for food and money. The father, in the meantime, also wandered around looking for his son.

Several years had passed, and the father's money had also run out. He decided to settle down in a large city in the kingdom of Magadha. With a combination of hard work and good luck, he achieved great success in business and became fabulously wealthy. He now lives in a large mansion, served by many hired hands, and his business continues to thrive. He is respected by all in the city and even enjoys the king's friendship. In spite of the wealth and the respect he had earned, he could not forget his son and he had no peace in his heart. "It has been fifty years since my foolish son disappeared," he said to himself, "I have riches beyond anyone's wildest dreams. I am old now, but I have no child to whom I can pass this wealth."

One day, the son was near his father's mansion by chance. He was looking for someone who might give him some food. He stood before the beautiful gate draped with magnificent fabrics and the portico sprinkled with numerous petals of fragrant and colorful flowers. There he saw an elderly man seated on a chair made of glittering gold, silver and precious stones, surrounded by many servants. The son did not recognize his father and thought he had come to the wrong place. "This mansion must belong to a prince or a prime minister. I have nothing to do with a place like this," he said to himself and moved on.

The father, however, recognized him from a distance. "Finally, my long-lost son has been found. O, how often have I dreamt of this moment!" he said to himself. He quickly sent his servants to fetch the son, but, frightened of the brawny men sent by his father, his son screamed and ran, then fainted and collapsed. The father realized his wealth overwhelmed his son. Pouring cold water on his face, the father decided not to reveal his true identity. He let the frightened son go back to the poor section of the city where he would be more comfortable.

The following day, the father sent two of his least impressive-looking servants and let them tell his son to come to work for him. "If he asks you what job I want him to do, tell him to clear the heap of dirt and clean the latrines." The son now felt a little more at ease and agreed to come to work for him.

The son now lives in a shack near his father's mansion. The father disguises himself as a poor old man and goes to see his son every day and teaches him many things gently and patiently. Many years have passed, and the son is now an educated and respectable man. The father, very old and ill now, tells him, "I know you to be an honest and worthy servant. I want to give you all I have. Will you accept it?" The son, still unaware of his master's true identity, refuses the offer, saying that a mere servant should not have such an honor. The father is impressed with his son's modesty, unspoiled by the education he gave him. When the time of his death finally approaches, he calls the son to his bedroom and holds his hand in the presence of the king and the dignitaries of the city, saying to them, "Listen to me, my dear friends. I want to reveal a secret. This man here is my true son and I am his true father. He left my home as a young man, but he has now come home. I am leaving all my assets to him, as he is my wise and worthy heir."

The sutra continues and says that the Buddha made us, though unworthy, his heirs and left us the true treasure of wisdom.

✦✦✦✦✦✦✦

The story comes from the Saddharma Pundarika Sutra,[26] commonly known as the Lotus Sutra. Written in the first century CE, probably in Kashmir, it has been one of the most popular sutras in Japan since its debut in the sixth century. The perceptive readers must have noticed the story's resemblance to the biblical parable of the Prodigal Son.[27] Both the Pundarika and the Prodigal Son stories describe the divine being as a compassionate and merciful father and imply that we are all his defiant and wayward children whose return the father awaits.

The most significant difference between the two parables is that the father in the Pundarika story educates his son slowly and patiently until he was made wise enough to be worthy of the gift prepared for him, while the father in the Prodigal Son story runs out to him the moment he recognizes the son, embraces him and showers on him the gift of love lavishly and unconditionally. Whether the son's moral disposition is worthy of the father's love is not even

---

[26] _Hokke-kyo_ [_Shinge-bon_] (Iwanami, Tokyo, Japan 1960) pp. 225-254. The text is also available on the Internet at www.sacred-texts.com/bud/lotus. _Pundarika_ means "white lotus."

[27] Luke 15:11-32

questioned. The fact that the long-lost son has returned is a reason enough for the father to rejoice and celebrate. The restored relationship with the son is more valued than the son's worthiness. At the same time, the father's aim now is to bring about reconciliation between the two sons, and the father's unconditional love is to serve as a model for the two sons' reconciliation and for all other human relationships.

On the other hand, the emphasis in the Pundarika parable is on the father's patient effort to inculcate wisdom in the son. The father's love for his son in the Pundarika story is perhaps as strong as father's love in the Prodigal Son story, but they manifest themselves in two different ways — one as an immediate and lavish outpouring of love and the other as a patient and careful expression of love. Perhaps they are the two aspects of divine compassion. The two strains of thought have been maintained in the Buddhist tradition to this day; while the Pure Land tradition focuses on the unconditional compassion of Amida Buddha, Zen focuses on attaining wisdom and illumination. In the Christian tradition, however, the father's unconditional love is more clearly pronounced, and the Gnostic movement, which represented the wisdom aspect of the faith, has been rejected as heretical, although there has been a renewed interest in the early Gnostic literature since the discovery of the Nag Hammadi Library.

Chapter Four:

Freedom of the Spirit

To master the art of Haiku,
learn all its rules diligently,
and forget them all.
　　— Matsuo Basho

The Bald-Headed Fool

$\mathcal{T}$he period between the late twelfth century and the middle of the thirteenth century in Japan's history was marked by unprecedented political upheavals, social unrest, and recurring famines, but it was also a time of great spiritual awakening and radical religious reforms. The early Buddhist alliance with the Imperial government appeared to have strengthened the religion at first, but it had, in time, weakened it and corrupted it. Several great spiritual leaders, such as Honen, Shinran, Dogen and Nichiren emerged and challenged the traditional teachings of the politically powerful, yet spiritually stagnant, Buddhism. Relying no longer on the patronage of the powerful but only on the authenticity of their spiritual insights, the reformers established the foundations of most of the Buddhist sects active in Japan today. Among them was Shinran, who founded the Jodo Shin School, the largest active Buddhist school in the world today.

Shinran was born in 1173 to a relatively low ranking aristocratic family in Kyoto. At the age of nine, he renounced the world and entered the monastery of Enryakuji Temple atop Mount Hiei for religious and academic training. One can only speculate what might have been the real reason for his entry into monastic life at such a tender age. With the emergence of warrior clans and the decline of aristocracy, his family may have felt that priesthood might give him a better future than aristocracy. At any rate, Shinran remained in the monastery for twenty years. In spite of the rigor in discipline, he found himself still unable to overcome his earthly desires and impure thoughts. Deeply disappointed at himself as well as the teaching of the Tendai School, he left Mt. Hiei at the age of twenty-nine and went to the venerable master Honen, who was teaching the Pure Land philosophy at Yoshimizu in Kyoto. Honen taught that one's salvation could be attained simply by reciting *Namu Amida Butsu* to invoke the compassion of Amida Buddha. Through Honen's instruction, Shinran came to realize for himself that if one cannot rely on one's own righteousness or enlightenment (Self Power) for salvation, one has no choice but to turn to the Buddha's compassion (Other Power). That was the heart of the Pure Land teaching. He no longer pretended to be or to become a righteous person, but honestly acknowledged his humanity and learned to place his complete trust in Amida Buddha's Vow of Compassion.

The rapid growth of Honen's Pure Land Buddhism did not sit well with the traditional Buddhist authorities. They not only criticized Honen for discarding the traditional Buddhist teachings and discipline, but also persuaded the Imperial Court to ban Honen's teachings altogether and banish him and his top disciples to distant Provinces. Honen was, thus, exiled to Tosa in the South at the age of 80, and Shinran to Echigo in the frigid North at the age of 34. They were also stripped of their priestly credentials and privileges. Shinran, the aristocratic scholar-priest, had never before had to earn his living by hard labor, but in Echigo, he lived as an ordinary man, tilling the land with his own hands for the first time. While in Echigo, he married a local woman, Eshin-ni, and had children. He learned there that one did not have to renounce the world to experience true liberation; liberation could be found in the midst of life in the world.

He was pardoned when he was thirty-nine, but the helplessness and hardships of life he experienced in Echigo only radicalized his faith in Amida Buddha's Compassion. "It does not matter whether my next life is found in the hell or in the paradise," said Shinran. "The only thing that matters to me is that I completely trust in Amida's Vow of

Compassion and thrust myself into his bosom of unconditional compassion. It's as simple as that."

A few years after he was pardoned, Shinran decided to relocate to the Eastern Provinces of Japan to spread the teachings of Other Power there. When he and his family were at Sanuki in the Province of Kozuke on their way to Eastern Japan, Shinran resolved to recite the Triple Pure Land Sutras one thousand times for the salvation of all sentient beings. A few days later, however, he stopped the recitation as he realized that what he was trying to do was to complement Amida's compassion with his own effort. He knew that the only thing necessary for salvation was to remember the compassion of Amida and to recite *Namu Amida Butsu*, yet he was trying to add extra merit to insure the salvation of others. He also realized that the only way to repay the compassion of the Amida Buddha was to trust in it himself and to help others do the same. In other words, he had temporarily lapsed into the old habit of Self Power. In 1231, when he became very ill with fever, he began to recite the Larger Pure Land Sutra. When he closed his eyes, however, he could see each letter of the sutra very clearly as if it was illuminated. "How strange!" he thought to himself. Then he remembered what happened at Sanuki seventeen years earlier. He stopped the recitation and he soon became well again. There should have been nothing on his mind but complete trust in and gratitude for Amida's compassion. Anything else would be a relapse into Self Power. The incident was recorded in his wife Eshin-ni's letter to their daughter. Eshin-ni recognized the special significance of the incident. It reminded Shinran how easy it was to go back to Self Power and how important it was to trust in Amida Buddha's compassion alone. He stayed in Eastern Japan for twenty years to spread the teachings of Other Power, after which he returned to Kyoto, where he lived the remainder of his life.

Shinran's teaching was later collected by his disciple, Yuien, in a book entitled *Tannisho (Notes Lamenting Differences)*, in which he said:

> *Even a good person can be born in the Pure Land, how much more so an evil person! However, people commonly say, "Even an evil person can be born in the Pure Land, how much more so a good person!" This may sound reasonable, but it is contrary to the intent of Other Power, the power of the [Amida Buddha's] Original Vow [of Compassion]. The reason for this is that those who believe that they themselves have the power to perform good acts are not inclined to rely completely on Other Power. Thus they are not in accord with the Original Vow of Amida. However, if they abandon their attachment to Self Power and entrust themselves completely to Other Power, then they, too, will be born in the True Land of Recompense.*

(*Tannisho*, Chapter 3)[28]

Conventional wisdom tells us that a good and righteous person will enjoy his or her rewards, while an evil person must suffer punishments. However, Shinran rejected this moralistic notion of the traditional teaching. He claimed that salvation was not a result of one's righteousness or ability to reach the enlightenment but of the Buddha's Compassion alone. It reminds us of the words of St. Paul, who wrote, "Since all have sinned and fall short of the glory of God, they are now justified by God's grace as a gift, through the redemption that is in Christ Jesus" (Romans 3:23-24).

Three hundred years before Martin Luther's Reformation, Shinran had already established the principles of "Grace alone" and "Faith alone." Works of righteousness may merit the person who performs them, but grace, when

---

[28] Bloom, Alfred, *Strategies for Modern Living – A Commentary with the Text of the Tannisho,* Numata Center, Berkeley, 1992, p. 4

received in faith, will liberate us all from the futile effort to prove ourselves worthy of salvation.

"Worthiness" is a relative concept, and, as such, it is based on comparison. On the other hand, "salvation" cannot be based on a relative thing like one's "worthiness" if it is to be truly universal. Therefore, it must rely on something more certain than human goodness or righteousness. For Shinran, it was Amida's compassion. He said, "Just utter the words *Namu Amida Butsu* (Adoration to Amida Buddha), and you know you are embraced in Amida's compassion."

Eventually, Shinran began to sign off all his writings with "Bald-Headed Fool." This was not an expression of his self-degradation, but of the joy of being liberated from having to prove his worthiness. His faith in Amida Buddha's Vow of Compassion made him free to admit his foolishness and joyfully proclaim it. After all, it is not our human excellence or righteousness that makes us worthy of salvation, but the compassion of the divine. Shinran would say to us, "You do not have to go through rigorous disciplines to become free from all your attachments. Just believe in and rely on God's grace, and you will be free — free to rejoice in your humanity and free to celebrate your foolishness and even your baldness."

Reflecting on Shinran's legacy, Dr. Alfred Bloom writes: "Shinran imbibed the spirit of Mahayana Buddhism. His Pure Land teaching is an inclusive, humane faith. It is non-authoritarian, non-dogmatic, egalitarian, non-superstitious religious faith. Through deepening religious understanding it liberates people from religious intimidation and oppression, which trade on the ignorance of people and their desire for security. Shinran's teaching does not encourage blind faith at the expense of one's reason and understanding."[29]

---

[29] Bloom, Alfred, *The Essential Shinran: A Buddhist Path of True Entrusting,* World Wisdom Inc., Bloomington, Indiana, 2007, p. 7

The Beloved Eccentric

Zen monk Ikkyu was born in 1394 as an illegitimate son of Emperor Go-Komatsu. His mother, who had left the palace by the time he was born, feared that his half-brothers might try to harm him, for he, too, had a claim to the Imperial throne. The only way to prove that he had no such ambition was to publicly renounce the world by becoming a priest. Thus, she sent him to Antokuji Temple in Kyoto to prepare him for priesthood. At the tender age of six, he had to sever his family ties and began a serious Zen training. Even as a child, he was known for his exceptional quick-wittedness and irreverent sense of humor. Among many anecdotes about his childhood, the following might be a good example of his irreverence and wit:

One day, Ikkyu saw his Zen master hide a jar of honey in a closet. "It is not fair for you to enjoy it by yourself, Master. I want some, too," he demanded. The master said, "This particular kind of honey is extremely poisonous if consumed by a child. It would certainly kill you." While the master was out on business, Ikkyu ate the honey to his heart's content. Then he took the master's most expensive antique bowl and smashed it into pieces. When the master returned and saw what had happened to his prized bowl, he was furious. Ikkyu calmly said, "I broke your precious bowl by mistake. I felt so badly that I decided to eat your honey to kill myself; but why hasn't it killed me?" Outsmarted by the child, the master was completely at a loss for words.

In 1416, Ikkyu sought instructions from Zen Master Kaso, who was one of the priests of prestigious Daitokuji

Temple, but lived alone in a little hut by Lake Biwa. Master Kaso first rejected Ikkyu, but moved by Ikkyu's persistence, he finally accepted Ikkyu as his disciple. Ikkyu was given the koan problem "Tozan's Sixty Blows" (*Gateless Gate*, Case 15),[30] and he is said to have solved it in 1418 at the age of twenty-five, when he was listening to a blind minstrel recite *The Tale of Heike*. Ikkyu continued his Zen training and an enlightenment finally came two years later, when he was on a boat meditating one dark night. In a state of deep meditation, he felt his mind, heart, body and all nature around him merge into one perfect harmony. Suddenly, a raven shrieked loudly, and at that moment, he was suddenly freed from all his earthly attachments and achieved his enlightenment. After a series of rigorous examinations by Master Kaso, he was given a certificate of enlightenment; but he immediately threw it into fire.

The Chinese-style poem he wrote upon his enlightenment went roughly like this:

> *Having lived a life of selfish dreams*
> *Arrogantly and angrily until now*
> *The raven's laughter cleared the dust off the seeker's illusion;*
> *Blissfully now I sing in the bright rays of the dawn.*

Completely freed from all worldly attachments now, his eccentricity only increased. He would make a mockery of

---

[30] When Tōzan came to study under Ummon, Ummon asked him, "Where are you from?" "From Sato," Tōzan replied. "Where were you during the summer?" "Well, I was at the monastery of Hōzu, south of the lake." "When did you leave there?" Ummon asked. "On August 25," was Tōzan's reply. "I spare you sixty blows," Ummon said. The next day Tōzan came to Ummon and said, "Yesterday you said you spared me sixty blows. I beg to ask you, where was I at fault?" "Oh, you rice bag!" shouted Ummon. "What makes you wander about, now west of the river, now south of the lake?" Tōzan thereupon came to a mighty enlightenment experience. (*Two Zen Classics – The Gateless Gate and The Blue Cliff Records,* translated by Katsuki Sekida, Shambhala, Boston, 2005, p. 61)

political powers and of religious authorities even more boldly.

When Ikkyu was in the Province of Ise, he was asked to conduct a dedicatory service to consecrate a new statue of Bodhisattva Jizo. The devotees of the benevolent Bodhisattva had gathered around the statue, adorned it with exquisite ornaments, and graced the entire shrine with the dignified aroma of incense. As they waited for the ceremony to begin, an air of solemnity surrounded the entire area. Ikkyu suddenly stood up, walked up to the statue, and urinated on it. He then turned to the people and said, "Now the statue has been duly consecrated," and left. The people were all astonished by this blasphemous act. It was indeed bizarre behavior, especially for a renowned priest! But by these absurd actions, Ikkyu was trying to expose the absurdity of religion's accepted practices. In this particular incident, he challenged not only their attachment to the lifeless statue, but all other idolatrous practices of institutional religion.

One day, a wealthy merchant asked for Ikkyu, now the famous abbot of Daitokuji Temple in Kyoto, to come to his mansion and conduct a service in commemoration of the anniversary of his parents' passing. Ikkyu came to the gate of the merchant's mansion barefooted and clad in rags, and announced, "I am here to pray for your parents' souls." The merchant thought he was a beggar and had his servants chase him away with sticks and stones. Later, when Ikkyu returned to the same mansion wearing the gold-brocaded satin vestment, a gift from the Imperial Court, the merchant came out to the gate to welcome him personally. After the service, the family served him an elaborate meal. Ikkyu said to the host, "When I came here an hour ago, you chased me away with sticks. You now welcome me with such lovely courtesy. The only difference seems to be this vestment. It appears that you value the vestment more than the person in it." Ikkyu took off his vestment and said, "This has no value to me, feel free to keep it," and left the mansion.

In Ikkyu's time, the country was not only undergoing the bloodiest civil war in the nation's history, but also suffering from droughts, famines, pestilences, and peasant revolts. Neither the political authorities nor the religious leaders took seriously their duties of bringing peace and healing to the nation. While tens of thousands were dying of starvation in Kyoto, the nobles were enjoying their sumptuous banquets, the warriors were fighting for dominance, and the priests were boasting their lofty scholarship, all in complete disregard of the suffering of the poor. Ikkyu's eccentricity, therefore, was an indictment to the hypocrisy of the powerful. His was a religion of the streets. The Imperial Court appointed him the Forty-Seventh Abbot of the prestigious Daitokuji Temple of Kyoto. He reluctantly accepted the appointment but refused to live within the walls of the temple precincts. Nothing could contain him. He was said to have been found often in a house of ill repute, writing romantic poems. Yet, he remained the most respected and beloved spiritual leader of his time, and people have not since stopped talking and writing about him.

ॐॐॐॐॐॐॐ

Ikkyu was the most eccentric of all the Buddhist priests I have ever heard of, but his eccentricity was rooted deeply in his inner sense of freedom and the conviction that all things are impermanent and have no substance. In his mind, all things are relative, including political powers, wealth, religious institutions and their moral teachings. No one should be bound by them as if they were absolute. That was what Ikkyu preached and practiced.

St. Paul declared, "For freedom Christ has set us free; stand fast therefore, and do not submit ever again to a yoke of slavery" (Galatians 5:1). I know we have been made free, completely free, by God's redeeming and liberating presence, but we still find ourselves bound by so many irrelevant forces. I know I could not possibly be the free-spirited eccentric that Ikkyu was, but I can learn to act on my freedom in ways that are possible for me.

Incidentally, the name Ikkyu means "a restful break." We find in his life a restful break from the world of attachments, anxieties and fear, as he brings to our awareness the fundamental freedom of spirit.

৵৵৵৵৵৵৵

Gasp,
laugh.

Grasp,
release.

Freedom's breath.

— Patricia Heinicke, Jr.

The Generous Pauper

$\mathcal{Z}$en monk Ryōkan (1758-1831) was a gentle hermit. Though he was renowned as a great poet, masterful in both Chinese and Japanese styles of poetry, and arguably one of the best calligraphers of his time, he dedicated himself to a solitary life of meditation in a tiny hut in the snowy mountains of Northern Japan. He renounced fame and material comfort and lived a pauper's life.

Ryōkan was a recluse, but not an escapist. He had no temple of his own, but at his small hut called Gogō-an (A Half Cup of Rice Hermitage), he received visitors freely. He was not a preacher, but through his poetry he touched many lives in a profound way. Whenever he was asked, he would write a few lines of poetry on whatever piece of paper was available and give it away. His hand-written poems became so popular that even during his lifetime many imitations were bought and sold for high prices in the urban art market, although he was oblivious to all that was happening in big cities. His poetry reflects three things: the joy of a simple way of life, compassion for all living beings — particularly for children and the poor — and love for nature. These three virtues constitute a very pertinent model for all of us today as we seek a lifestyle that can sustain our natural environment as well as peace in the world.

One evening, a burglar broke into Ryōkan's hut. Ryōkan felt so badly about having nothing for the man that he took his robe off and gave it to the disappointed burglar. When the burglar left the hut, Ryōkan saw the moonlight shining into his room through the window, which the burglar had used to make his escape. Feeling sorry for the burglar who could not take the moon with him, he wrote:

A burglar failed to carry off the moon.
It now shines in through the window.
How beautiful!

Though he owned nothing, he had the rich beauty of nature to enjoy; the magnificence of the moonlight was enough to make him feel exceedingly rich. This spirituality was a reflection of the harmony of the universe. To Ryōkan, nature was not something to conquer and exploit, but something to live in harmony with. Just as he refused to fight his karma, he refused to alienate himself from the law of nature. All things in nature were his friends. He even tried to remove the roof of his hut to allow the bamboo shoot that came through his floor to grow without being hampered. He felt compassion toward a solitary black pine drenched in the cold rain, and wrote:

The poor little pine tree,
standing alone in the middle of the field at Iwamuro
on this cold, rainy day,
if you were a man, I would let you borrow my umbrella,
I would even put my straw raincoat on your shoulders.

Ryōkan loved to play with the village children. When he played hide-and-seek with them one day, he hid himself so well in the haystack that no one was able to find him. Even after the children were long gone, he would not come out, thinking they were still looking for him. He stayed there all night until he was discovered by a farmer the next morning. "Reverend Ryōkan, what are you doing here?" asked the peasant. "Hush. Not so loud, the children might find me," was Ryōkan's response.

The children of the village and I
played ball all day long,
wishing this Spring day with them
would never come to an end.

In the mendicant tradition of Buddhist monks, Ryōkan would go out to the village from time to time with a begging bowl in his hand to receive alms. But if he met a beggar on his way home, he would give away everything he had. By doing so, he was not trying to perform "good deeds." It was a purely spontaneous response on his part. In other words, he merely lived out his natural impetus to share whatever he had with the poor. As far as he was concerned, even such a deed was part of nature.

> *If this black priestly robe of mine*
> *was big enough,*
> *I would have embraced all the poor in the world*
> *under my sleeves.*

When Ryōkan was seventy years of age, a thirty-year-old nun, Teishin, came to visit him. While she was looking for a good Zen master for her own training, she came across Ryōkan's poems and found in them a truly enlightened spirit. Despite the forty year difference between them, they quickly fell in love with each other. They saw each other only a few times, but exchanged love poems when they were apart. Four years later, in December, he became seriously ill. He was hoping to last through the winter so that he could see her again, but she did not wait for the end of the winter; she braved the frozen pass to come to see him. Relieved to see her, Ryōkan wrote:

> *The one I have been waiting to see so long has come;*
> *Not a care in my heart!*

He knew his days were numbered, and gave her another short verse:

> *The maple leaf is falling,*
> *showing both the front and the back.*

This was his way of telling her that he had lived his life as if he had nothing to hide, and he had no regrets. A few days later, he quietly breathed his last. Teishin was given the responsibility of collecting and editing Ryōkan's poems into an anthology, which she entitled *Dews on the Lotus Flowers.*

If he was alive today, Ryōkan would say to us, "Consume less and share more. Know that the future of the planet depends on it. What you own does not make you rich. How can anybody own the beauty of nature that makes your life so rich? Treat creation with respect and care. Treat every person you meet with respect and care also."

The very last poem he wrote before he died at the age of seventy-four was this:

As my inheritance I deed to you, my friends,
        springtime flowers, mountain cuckoos,
and autumn's bright maple leaves.

Zingiber Mioga

My favorite vegetable is *myoga*, also known among botanists as *zingiber mioga*. Unlike its more famous relative, ginger, only the pink part of its crunchy stem is eaten. It has a very refreshing taste and a pleasant aroma. The word *myoga* consists of two Chinese characters: *myo*, meaning "name," and *ga*, "carry." Put together, it means "Carrying one's name." My stepmother used to say, "*Myoga* is delicious, but eating too much of it will make you forgetful." "Why?" I asked. "I don't know, but my grandmother used to tell me that," was her reply. I could not think of any reason why it should make us forgetful. A few years later, however, I came across a story that may have originated the popular belief.

Among the Buddha's disciples was a very forgetful one, according to the story. He would forget anything and everything the Enlightened One had taught him. Not only that, he would even forget a simple thing like his own name. Since the Buddha was compassionate and understanding, he wrote the disciple's name on a piece of paper and had him hang it from his neck.

Realizing the disciple's lack of aptitude for academics, the Buddha assigned him to the simple daily task of sweeping a garden. When he was raking the fallen leaves one autumn morning, his broom struck a little rock. It rolled a few yards and stopped. At that very moment, he attained the enlightenment. He became one of the most respected and beloved among all of the Buddha's disciples. Years later, this saintly man died, and from the mound under which he was buried sprouted a strange looking plant. His friends named it *myoga* in honor of him who always had to carry his own name. Perhaps his friends ate too much of it; none of them remembered to tell their posterity what his real name was. But the ability to forget the things that are not essential, along with the simplicity of his faith and the depth of his enlightenment, still lives in the plant known as *zingiber mioga*.

ॐॐॐॐॐॐॐ

The story reminds us that the ability to forget may be a great gift of freedom. It may enable us to focus on what is truly important. There are many things we must forget so that we may be able to move on without the burden of painful memories.

ॐॐॐॐॐॐॐ

"Forgetting what lies behind and straining forward to what lies ahead, press on toward the goal for the prize of the heavenly call of God in Christ Jesus" — Philippians 3:13-14

"See, former things have come to pass, and new things I now declare" — Isaiah 42:9

Echoing the prophet's words, the author of the Book of Revelation wrote to the believers under persecution, *"Behold, I am making all things new"* (Revelation 21:5). Instead of remaining a product of the past, we can be a new creation for God's new world.

Bodhidharma

On September 21, 520 CE, a man with a striking appearance stepped out of a junk and landed on the shore of southern China. The wild-eyed, profusely bearded man had brown skin and an enormous head. The earliest mentions of him in the Chinese texts described him as a "blue-eyed barbarian" and a "Central Asian from Persia." Apparently, they did not know what to make of him. He was actually a Buddhist monk who had just completed his three year voyage from India. His name was Bodhidharma. He was born a prince in southern India, but in a single-minded quest for enlightenment, he renounced the world and became a monk. After many years of studying, training and meditation under the guidance of Prajnatara, he attained enlightenment and became a renowned master of the Dharma (Buddhist teachings). He then decided to travel to China to propagate Buddhism there.

The Emperor Wu of Liang, one of the southern Chinese dynasties, was a devoted Buddhist. When he heard of the arrival of a learned monk from India, he invited him to the palace, hoping to hear from him some edifying words.

"I have built monasteries and temples, recruited many brilliant men and women into priesthood, and have studied and copied many sacred scriptures myself. How much karmic merit have I earned from all these things I have done?" asked the Emperor.

Bodhidharma uttered just one word, "Nothing."

"Why so?" the Emperor inquired.

"One may marvel at these impressive temples and monasteries, but they are all illusions, no-entities. The true merit comes from pure wisdom beyond the grasp of human intelligence, and it is not attainable by way of reason or good deeds."

Puzzled by the answer he heard, the Emperor asked him, "Who is the man standing before me?"

"I do not know," was the reply.

Offended by the monk's defiant responses, the Emperor banned his strange teaching. Equally offended was Bodhidharma to find that Buddhism in China had been reduced to earning karmic merits and conducting empty rituals instead of seeking true wisdom and nirvana. Disappointed, Bodhidhama set out again. He crossed the Yangze River to the north and came to Shaolin Temple in the northern kingdom of Wei. He then went into a cave near the temple and sat in silence facing the wall for the next nine years.

In the meantime, many students of Buddhism visited Shaolin seeking instructions from Bodhidharma, but he rejected all of them until a young Confucian scholar named Hui-ke came to Shaolin. As he did to all others before him, the reclusive master rejected him several times. Hui-ke resorted to a drastic measure; he cut off his arm to show his determination. Surprised by this, Bodhidharma finally gave in and accepted him as a disciple. Eventually, Dao-yu, Tai-Fu and Tsung-Chi (a nun) also came under Bodhidharma's tutelage.

When Bodhidharma knew he was about to die, he called his disciples to his side to test their attainments. He asked each of them, "What is truth?"

Tai-Fu said, "Truth transcends yes and no. It moves."

The master said, "Tai-Fu, you have my skin."

Tsung-Chi said, "It is like Ananda's view of the Buddha Realm. Seen once, and never seen again."

The master said, "Tsung-Chi, you have my flesh."

Dao-yu said, "The four elements are all void; the five constituents of form, sensation, conception, cognition, and consciousness are also void. There is nothing to be grasped as real."

The master said, "Dao-yu, you have my bone."

When his turn came, Hui-ke bowed to the master and stood there without a word.

The master said, "Hui-ke, you have my marrow."

Bodhidharma thus made Hui-ke the Second Patriarch of Zen in China.

The transmission of Patriarchal Authorities in Zen was granted by the master only to the disciple who had mastered the marrow of the master's teaching. Since Zen is outside the scriptural authorities and does not rely on letters, the mastery of Zen cannot be measured by objective standards. It is a totally intuitive process.

According to The Anthology of the Patriarchal Hall (952 CE), when Bodhidharma died, his disciple Hui-ke placed him in a casket and laid him to rest in a tomb in Mt. Xiong'er. Three years later, when Song-yun, a royal envoy of one of the northern dynasties, was crossing the frozen Pamir Mountains on his way home to China, he met a strange-looking Indian monk. He said he was on his way back to India. Song-yun thought it strange that the monk was wearing a sandal on one foot but nothing on the other. The Indian monk told Sang-yun that his emperor had just passed away. Upon his arrival back in China, The royal envoy learned that his emperor had indeed been dead. When he checked his diary, he found, to his astonishment, that the date of the emperor's death coincided with the day when he met the stranger in the Pamir Mountains. Curious about the identity of the man who knew what he could not have known, Song-yun began to inquire about the mysterious monk. Someone suggested to him, "The only Indian priest known to possess such powers was Bodhidharma, but he has been dead for three years." Song-yun went to Mt. Xiong'er and had Bodhidharma's tomb reopened, and found it empty. There was, however, a single sandal remaining in the tomb.

࿔࿔࿔࿔࿔࿔࿔

The life of Bodhidharma was shrouded in the cloud of mystery. Some scholars doubt he even existed, yet his powerful influence is still felt today among those who practice Zen meditation. We may not know much about his life or his background, but we do know that he shunned any display of scholarship or status, and developed simple ways of reaching intuitive recognition of the Buddha-nature within. In other words, he established the basic format of Zen meditation.

The story of Bodhidharma's mysterious appearance to the Chinese official in the Pamir Mountains three years after his death is intriguing. What is interesting to me is that the story consists of two elements — the empty tomb and the post-resurrection appearance, just like the accounts of Christ's resurrection. What is more interesting is the fact that, while Christ's resurrection was, and still is, a source of profound inspiration to all Christians, the story of Bodhidharma's resurrection does not seem to be anything more than an incidental anecdote. In the belief system that assumes the soul's interminable cycles of reincarnation, death was never considered final anyway. Because there is no finality attached to death, resurrection would have no particular significance. Christ's resurrection, on the other hand, is more than an incidental anecdote of a great man. To be honest, it does not matter to me whether it was a bodily resurrection or a spiritual one. What is important to me is that, in spite of the terrible death he died on the cross, it was not the end; a new life emerged out of the tomb, and his life keeps renewing ours whenever we face an end. An end always turns out to be a new beginning. We see in Christ's death and resurrection a radical discontinuity overcome by redemptive synthesis, and the world of dualities overtaken by the primordial unity.

Just as the teaching of karma has helped the people of the Eastern religious traditions face their hardships with dignity and moral uprightness, the teaching of *samsara* (reincarnation or a soul's endless transmigration) has helped many of them face death without an exaggerated sense of finality, but I am not sure how many Buddhist and Hindu scholars today are taking it seriously. I, for one, find it difficult to believe that I am going to be reborn as another person or animal or an insect after this life ends. I feel this life on earth is a part of something infinitely greater, but I hesitate to call it *samsara*.

Eternity is not the same as endlessness. An endless extension of time does not constitute eternity. Eternity is that which transcends time. It is something that can be experienced right at this moment. Actually, Buddhists seek to be freed from the endless rebirths of *samsara* and to find themselves in a blissful peace of nirvana. What all of us are striving for is to transcend this chronological time and have a glimpse of eternity, because once you have a glimpse of eternity, time, in a chronological sense, becomes irrelevant, and each moment in life begins to assume its eternal quality. Christ's resurrection, to me, makes it possible to transcend the chronological time and to see eternity.

The Sixth Patriarch

*H*ui-neng (A.D. 638-713) was born in Hsin-chou in southern China. His father's untimely death left his family so poor that young Hui-neng had to work long hours every day as a firewood vender to help his mother. As a result, he never had an opportunity to learn to read or write.

One day, when he was out in town selling firewood, he heard a man recite the Diamond Sutra. The words of the sutra touched Hui-neng so profoundly that a deep aspiration was awakened in his heart to study the sutra under a great master. As soon as an arrangement was made to care for his aging mother, he set out on a month-long journey to Yellow Plum Mountain in Northern China, where Hung-jen, the Fifth Patriarch of Zen Buddhism, lived and taught among his disciples.

When Hui-neng paid homage to Hung-jen at the monastery, the patriarch asked Hui-neng, "Where did you come from?" "I came from Hsin-chou," replied Hui-neng. "So you are a southern aborigine. What do you want?" "I want to become a Buddha," replied Hui-neng. "You cannot become a Buddha; southern aborigines have no Buddha-nature," said the patriarch. Undaunted by the master's blunt remark, Hui-neng rebutted, "Whether one belongs to the southern or northern race is of no consequence as far as Buddha-nature is concerned. Our difference is only in physical appearance." The patriarch was impressed with Hui-neng's defiant spirit, but afraid to appear too friendly to the uneducated southerner, the master told him to work in the rear.

Eight months later, when the Patriarch felt it was time to choose his successor, he ordered all his disciples to submit a verse, with which he would determine who among his disciples had the most authentic understanding of his teaching. Now, among Hung-jen's disciples was Shin-shau, well known for his sound learning and exceptional intelligence. The rest of the disciples refused to enter the contest because it was clear to them that none of them could match Shin-shau's caliber anyway. Under the circumstance, Shin-shau himself hesitated to submit his verse. But his desire to have his understanding tested was so great that he waited until midnight and secretly wrote on the wall of the corridor the following verse:

Our body is the Bodhi-tree,
and our mind a mirror bright.
Carefully we cleanse and watch them hour by hour,
and let no dust collect upon them.

Next morning, having read this anonymous stanza, Master Hung-jen ordered all his disciples to memorize it and recite it. In the meantime, Hui-neng was hulling rice in the rear, unaware of the events unfolding in the monastery. When a young monk walked by, reciting the verse out loud, Hui-neng stopped him and asked him what it was about. Upon hearing the young monk's account, Hui-neng persuaded the reluctant monk to write on the same wall Hui-neng's own version:

By no means is our body a Bodhi-tree,
Nor is the mind a mirror bright.
Since mind is emptiness,
Where can the dust collect?

When the patriarch saw this, he immediately knew that those words were Hui-neng's and that the uneducated Southerner was the one ready to succeed his office, but the whole monastery was enraged at the lowly rice-huller's challenge to the established reputation of Shin-shau. That night, the master gave Hui-neng private instruction on The

Diamond Sutra and secretly passed the robe, the insignia of the patriarch's office, to Hui-neng. At the advice of his master, Hui-neng immediately left the mountain to elude the agitated monks and went into hiding. A few years later, Hui-neng emerged as a prominent Zen master in the South. Thousands of students flocked around him seeking to learn from his wisdom. More than one and a half centuries after Bodhidharma brought the new school of Buddhism from India to China, the Zen movement finally reached its Golden Age under the guidance of the illiterate man, Hui-neng of Hsin-chou, the Sixth Patriarch.

ৡৡৡৡৡৡৡ

Shin-shau's verse refers to the "mind" that requires watchful attention and constant cleansing, while Hui-neng's to the "Mind" itself. As long as our spiritual discipline is focused only on keeping our minds clean, we are still preoccupied with "our" minds. Such an effort usually results either in self-righteous satisfaction or heartbreaking disappointment. It is true that much of the Zen training consists in learning to control one's own breath, mind, and body, but true liberation cannot be achieved until we surrender our minds to the Mind that is Emptiness itself.

Shin-shau, the intellectual elite of his time, was unable to free himself from the accepted assumptions and sentiments of his culture, while illiterate Hui-neng was able to penetrate straight into the heart of the teaching.

Later, when the Fifth Patriarch, Hung-jen, was asked why he chose Hui-neng as his successor, Hung-jen's answer was: "Because that man doesn't understand Buddhism at all." In an analytical sense, Hui-neng, perhaps, did not understand Buddhism at all, but he was able to grasp intuitively the most central, yet most elusive, wisdom *(prajna)* of its teaching.

⤳⤳⤳⤳⤳⤳⤳

Some of our civilization's assumptions and prejudices can obscure what is authentic and undermine what is true. Our logic assumes the distinction between subject and object, and our religious sentiment demands the separation of the sacred from the secular. Thus, our "educated" minds are hopelessly tied to all sorts of dualistic assumptions, and our propensity toward utilitarian rationalism clutters an intuitive discernment of life's inmost mystery. We are moving farther and farther away from the blissful ignorance of Adam and Eve before they ate from the tree of knowing good and evil.

Knowing something requires a discriminating mind. With a discriminating mind, we can tell the difference between a cherry blossom and a plum blossom, for instance. But when a cherry blossom falls to the ground, it is decomposed by some microorganisms in the ground and becomes small organic elements in the soil. Suppose a plum tree next to the cherry tree absorbs the organic elements that used to be a cherry blossom. Then, what used to be a cherry blossom is now seen as a plum blossom. In other words, our conventional, discriminating minds can only go so far and fail to see the deeper and more permanent reality of life in those two blossoms. At the level of our five senses and reason, the distinction between the two blossoms clearly exists, but it is impermanent; at the deeper, unconscious level of *alaya*,[31] the distinction ceases to be and a totally new, integrative perception begins. That is what Hui-neng was able to perceive.

"Knowing is unknowing," according to Hui-neng. The process of learning, therefore, is that of unlearning the duality of things.

---

[31] See the Introduction, page xix.

Comic Spirit

$\mathcal{A}$t almost every Oriental gift shop, customers are greeted by a statue of a pot-bellied monk with a broad smile on his face. The happy and guileless smile beaming from his entire corpulent body somehow manages to make even the most despondent smile a little. The curious statue is actually that of a late ninth century Zen monk called Pu-tai (or Hotei in Japanese). Since monastic life was too confining to him, he left the monastery and lived as a wayfaring mendicant monk. His name, Pu-tai, means "Linen Sack" in Chinese. He was so named because he always carried with him a linen sack, which contained all his possessions. Having renounced all his desires for worldly possessions and recognition, his religious exercise consisted almost entirely of playing with village children. He took a special delight in producing candies and toys from his famous linen sack and giving them to children. This jovial figure's roaring laughter is definitely one of the true faces of spiritual life.

તે તે તે તે તે તે તે

Religious people, by and large, tend to be too serious. In Zen, however, a sense of humor is considered an integral part of its spirituality. Once people have attained their enlightenment, they are no longer attached to anything. They are not only free from the world of vanity and impermanence, but from their own self-importance also. Thus, they do not take themselves seriously; sometimes, they do not even take the Buddha seriously. It is in this context that we must understand Zen Master Lin-Chi's curiously impious words, "If you meet the Buddha, kill him."

A sense of humor is the ability to laugh at oneself even in the most somber of situations. As G.K. Chesterton reminded us, "The reason why the angels can fly is that they take themselves so lightly." When we are too preoccupied with our own agenda, we have no room for the truly amusing and comical aspects of life that we are perhaps meant to receive as God's gift.

When the eighth century Zen monk Teng Yin-Feng was dying, he asked his friends, "I have seen monks die sitting and lying, but has anyone died standing?" "Yes, some," was the reply. "How about upside down?" he inquired. "We have never seen anyone die like that," they responded to the odd question. So Teng stood on his head and died. Even in his death, he exhibited his spiritual freedom from fear and anxiety by performing this comic relief.

☙☙☙☙☙☙☙

Hearty laughter is a sign of freedom within. Only out of a truly liberated mind comes a true recognition of what is amusing in the world. Thus, many of the Zen inspired poems observe what is ludicrous and laughable in life and express it in witty and humorous ways:

> *The two tiny baby creatures*
> *in the eyebrow of a mosquito*
> *never stop quarrelling between themselves*
> *as to whose earth this is.*
> — Hakuin[32]

---

[32] Hyers, Conrad *Zen and the Comic Spirit,* The Westminster Press, Philadelphia, 1974, p. 17

On how to sing
the frog school and the skylark school
are arguing.
                                        — Shiki[33]

ॐॐॐॐॐॐॐ

Here is Patricia's prayer about our inability to laugh at ourselves. I am sure all can identify with it.

I cannot laugh at myself because I am easily
offended because I am oversensitive because
I expect to be ridiculed because I assume

people despise me because I am not understood be-
cause
I do not open myself because
I expect to be ridiculed because I despise/
exalt myself as beyond understanding because
I carry a great pain that has not been recognized.

I cannot stop laughing...
I am small and filled with pain and when I look fear-
less at You
my pain melts into universal pain and
my defects join the throng of defects ...
bearable they are at last.
All forgiven, all is given, which
restores me to my Self and opens me to
Joy, and when I look in love to You
my loveliness joins the sky of loveliness and
my hilarity adds to Hilarity's roar.
                                — Patricia Heinicke, Jr.

---

[33] Ibid. p. 17

Chapter Five:

Healing and Wholeness

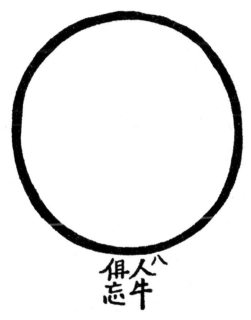

Then some people came, bringing to him a paralyzed man, carried by four of them. And when they could not bring him to Jesus because of the crowd, they removed the roof above him; and after having dug through it, they let down the mat on which the paralytic lay. When Jesus saw their faith, he said to the paralytic, "Son, your sins are forgiven." He said to the paralytic — "I say to you, stand up, take your mat and go to your home."

— Mark 2:3-5, 10b-12

Poppy Seeds

Once upon a time, a young mother lost her child. Her agony was so great that she wandered about like a madwoman, pleading with everyone, "Please! Bring my baby back to life!" The people tried to comfort her, but it was clear that nothing short of the child's miraculous resurrection would satisfy her. So they suggested to her, "Go to the forest outside the village, and find the man called Gotama the Buddha. He just might be the one who is able to bring your child back to life again." So, with her child's corpse in her arms, she went to see the Buddha and begged him to revive the child. He felt deep compassion for her and said, "I need to ask you to do something for me before I revive your child. Go back to the village and ask someone to give you some poppy seeds and bring them back to me." She thought to herself, "This is too easy; anyone would be able to spare me some poppy seeds." When she was about to leave, Gotama spoke again and said to her, "By the way, the poppy seeds I need for your child must come from someone who has not lost a loved one." Still thinking it would be easy, she went back to the village and began to visit the villagers' homes, one by one. Every one of them would be happy to give her what she asked for, but actually no one could, because everyone had lost someone very dear. The young mother finally began to understand what Gotama was trying to do. She returned to the forest and thanked him for the wise counsel he gave her.

Reviving the child might have temporarily eased the mother's agony, but it would not be a permanent solution to the problem of life's transience. As the young mother learned, all of us experience grief and sorrow many times over throughout our journey of life. All things are fleeting, and nothing is permanent. Whatever we have, we will certainly lose it eventually. Meeting is a beginning of parting. That seems to be the nature of life. Therefore, in this life, we must be always ready to let go of whatever we cherish. It does not mean, however, that we can no longer enjoy life's pleasures. Quite the contrary; we will be able to appreciate each moment of our lives more fully when we know it will never come back again.

❧❧❧❧❧❧❧

In *Chanoyu*, the Japanese art of tea ceremony, the most important lesson one must learn is that of *"Ichi-Go, Ichi-Ye,"* or "One Life, One Encounter." When you have a guest in your tea room, this lesson teaches, serve him or her your best cup of tea in the most hospitable way you possibly can, as if it was the very last cup of tea you can offer to your friend.

When you have a cup of tea with your friend, savor every sip of the tea and every word of your conversation. Appreciate the aroma of the tea, the warmth and the texture of the cup and even the sound it makes when you put it on the saucer. Above all, cherish every moment of your brief time with your friend, because, after all, it could very well be the last moment you share with him or her. Everything is impermanent. Nothing lasts forever. There may not be a next time. Even if there is a next time, it is not the same anymore, because what happens now can never be repeated.

Abbot Zenkei Shibayama of Nanzenji Temple of Kyoto wrote this poem, entitled "Flower Does Not Talk."

Silently, a flower blooms;
silently, it falls to the ground;
and it never returns to the tree.
Yet, at this moment and at this place

it fully reveals all the glories of the world.
The voice of a silent flower!
The truth of a single blossom!
The joy of eternal life that can never be destroyed
shines through it brilliantly with no regrets
whatsoever.

Each moment of life is precious, for it may very well be the last moment to enjoy. Each person you meet is precious, for he or she may very well be the last person you meet in your life. Everything passes and everything changes. Every moment is eschatological!

The Octopus Temple

About eight hundred years ago in the beautiful city of Kyoto, there was a young priest in training. His name was Zenko. An important part of the Buddhist training was to learn not to harm any living creature and keep a strict vegetarian diet. It was called the vow of *Ahimsa* (No-killing). He took the vow seriously and did not kill or harm any living thing. He was careful to not even step on an ant by mistake. But one day, he received word that his mother was seriously ill. With his superior's permission, he brought his dying mother to his living quarters in the temple so he could care for her. The young man asked her:

"Mother, is there anything you would like me to do for you while I am here with you? I love you so much, and I want to do something for you."

"Son, I have lived a long and good life and have been blessed with a good son like you. I have no regrets, except…"

"Except what, mother?"

"Except…Well, as you know, my favorite dish is a cooked octopus. I would like to be able to taste a slice of it before I die."

On account of the vow of *Ahimsa*, he could not kill. He agonized over it all night, but finally decided to break the vow for his mother. He knew it meant he would no longer be able to become a priest, but for the sake of his dying mother, he was willing to sacrifice his own aspiration for priesthood. He got up early in the morning, went to a fish market, bought an octopus and cooked it. The mother thanked him profusely after tasting a bite of her favorite dish.

"You have been very kind to me, son. You have given me so much love, much more than I ever deserved. I thank you. I love you so much. Now I can go in peace, with no regrets whatsoever."

A few nights after the mother's death, the Buddha himself appeared in Zenko's dream and said,

"You have done well, young man. You will become a great priest."

"But I have killed an octopus."

"Yes, you did. You broke the vow out of compassion for your dying mother. As a matter of fact, if you had refused to cook the octopus dish, which was your dying mother's last wish, I would have rejected your wish to become a priest. I would not want a priest who doesn't know there is something more important than a mere rule. You have the vow of *Ahimsa* so that you will learn the meaning of compassion. Many keep the vow, but never learn. You, on the other hand, have learned well. You acted compassionately. You will be able to guide my people well as a great priest."

The young man indeed became a respected priest and founded a temple. Because of the story, his temple came to be known as "The Octopus Temple."

ઌઌઌઌઌઌઌ

Roman Catholicism was first introduced to Japan by St. Francis Xavier in 1549. Despite the government's inconsistent reception, the church flourished there by the heroic effort of Jesuit and Franciscan missionaries from Portugal and Spain. In 1639, Christianity was banned altogether and the nation closed its doors to foreigners. The government's decision to disallow the missionary activities came when it sensed Europe's colonial ambition under the guise of the seemingly harmless Christian mission. All the foreign missionaries were expelled, and many believers were tortured and executed. During the Catholic heyday, however, there was a beautiful cathedral in Kyoto. I even knew roughly where it stood. When I had an opportunity to visit Kyoto, I went to see the site, which is now in the middle of a busy shopping area. At the place where the beautiful edifice once graced this ancient capital of Japan stands a Buddhist temple called Tako Yakushi, loosely translated "The Octopus Temple."

I went inside and asked if I could see a priest. Despite the fact that I had made no appointment, the priest was gracious enough to invite me in for a cup of tea and a little chat. That was when I learned the story of the Octopus Temple. I was disappointed that there was nothing to remind me of the Christian cathedral's once glorious edifice, but I knew that the spirit of Christ was alive and well in the story of the Octopus Temple. It is indeed a story of love and compassion.

ॐॐॐॐॐॐॐ

Join Patricia again in her prayer:

He relinquished his priestly vocation
for the sake of his mother's last craving
and became a great priest.

(If you let go of your desire for another's sake,
your desire will be restored to you.)

There are many such stories
in fable and in real lives.
I have seen this moral come to be,
but I always want to ask,
"Does it always work that way?

Is it guaranteed?"

*Of course, an insured letting go
is not really letting go.
Giving in order to gain
is not really sacrifice.
The moral would be only one more rule,
one more failed recipe for fulfillment.*

*Right? Then why tell us these stories?
Why encourage compassion by promising
restoration?
If you are not a god of recipes,
and not a god of harsh discipline,
might you be a God of outrageous generosity,
your free gifts teaching us to give?*

*I hesitate to believe it.
Help my hesitation.*

— Patricia Heinicke, Jr.

Mulian's Family

*A*mong the closest disciples of Gotama the Buddha, Shariputra was known for wisdom, Ananda for loyalty, and Purna for eloquence, but Mulian[34] was best known for his supernatural powers, with which he was able to ascend to the heavens and descend to the underworlds freely. He searched the whole universe for his deceased mother, and found her in the underworld of hungry ghosts, suffering from the unbearable agony of *Ullambana*. (The word *Ullambana* literally means "hung upside down" in Sanskrit and indicates the highest degree of suffering.) He naturally tried to rescue her from her suffering, but even his supernatural power was of no avail. He quickly went back to the Buddha and begged him to save her.

"Your mother is suffering in the netherworld as a result of what she did in her life; there is nothing I can do to undo it. She refused to feed the hungry and refused to give to the poor in spite of the great wealth she enjoyed; she did things only for herself while living," the Buddha said to Mulian. "If there is anything that can get her out of the agony of *Ullambana*, it would be your sacrificial offerings on her behalf as her son."

"What would be an appropriate sacrificial offering that might help her?" asked Mulian.

"My disciples will be completing their summer training on July 15. They will be hungry as they have been fasting. I suggest that you feed them when they come out of the retreat," the Buddha replied. Mulian, hence, prepared a special meal for

---

[34] Chinese name for Moggallana.

all his three thousand fellow disciples. After they enjoyed the meal, they all prayed for the release of Mulian's mother. On that very day, she was released from her *Ullambana* suffering.

To this day, the people of Japan observe a three day *Urabon* (Japanese for *Ullambana*) holiday in mid-August, which is close to July 15 of the old lunar calendar. They go home to their parents in commemoration of the release of Mulian's mother from her hellish suffering and pray for the peace and wellbeing of the souls of their deceased ancestors. They hang lanterns outside their homes and perform *Bon (Urabon)* dances to welcome the released spirits of the dead. Since so many people try to go home on the same day, the bumper-to-bumper traffic on the nation's freeway system is indeed horrific and is compared to the suffering of *Ullambana* itself.

Now, Mulian had a brother who was as greedy and selfish as his mother. Mulian told him about their mother and the consequences of greed, trying to make him change his ways. At first, he rejected Mulian's advice, saying, "The poor are poor because they are all lazy. They have no right to expect anything from me. As for me, I will enjoy the wealth I have earned." Mulian explained to him, "I know you have always made wise and prudent investments. Now consider this: a single deed of charity will multiply ten thousand times, and it will all be returned to you." The selfish brother thought it was the best investment opportunity he had ever heard of. He opened one of his warehouses and gave everything in it to the poor, and watched anxiously for his investment to multiply ten thousand times and come back to him. When he saw nothing returning to him, he was very upset and went back to Mulian and said,

"Mulian, you are a priest, and yet you lied to me."

"No, I did not lie to you."

"Why is it, then, that I have not seen any return for my investment?"

"It has been added to your account. I will show you if you don't believe me. Hang on to my robe."

As his brother held on to Mulian's robe, he flew upward at the speed of light. As they saw the lower heavens on their upward flight, Mulian's brother was impressed with how lovely they looked. When they reached the sixth heaven, Mulian stopped and let his brother explore a little on his own. He came across elegant heavenly ladies sewing beautiful robes.

"Noble ladies, you do not look like sewing ladies to me. Why and for whom are you sewing those beautiful robes?"

"These robes are for the Venerable Mulian's brother. We have been told that he emptied one of his treasure houses for the poor and will be reborn into the sixth heaven when his time comes. We are preparing for his arrival."

"My brother did not lie to me; this is far better than all my earthly treasures put together," he said.

When they returned to earth, Mulian's brother emptied all his warehouses and gave all his treasures to the poor and the hungry.

❧❧❧❧❧❧❧

The story reminds us of the words of Jesus:

"Do not store up for yourselves treasures on earth,
where moth and rust consume and where thieves
break in and steal;
but store up for yourselves treasures in heaven,
where neither moth nor rust consumes
and where thieves do not break in and steal.
For where your treasure is, there your heart will be
also.

(Matthew 6:19-21)

Both the biblical and the Buddhist traditions regard "storing up treasure in heaven" more highly than accumulating earthly wealth. This story is obviously intended to be a warning against greed, but it is a bit unsettling as a moral teaching because Mulian was assured of a heavenly reward while his motivation for emptying the warehouse for the poor was still greed. In other words, the story doesn't really deal with morality as a spiritual issue. Neither does it deal with the traditional Eastern concepts of causality (karma) and reincarnation *(samsara)* at a deeper level. While the story talks about a clear causal relationship between greed and future suffering and between the act of giving and its heavenly reward, it is a superficial, almost mechanical, application of the law of karma and *samsara*.

❧❧❧❧❧❧❧

The concepts of karma and *samsara* were not original to Buddhism; they came from the old traditional teachings of India. While the idea of karma seems to foster passivity and determinism, an aspect of it may represent a process of what C.G. Jung called "individuation," or the process in which the overwhelming force of the "archetypes" stored in our *alaya* unfolds itself through one's life. In other words, karma may be the collective unconscious formed through hundreds of thousands of years of human experiences trying to unfold in individual lives.

Samsara (reincarnation, or the endless transmigration of life/self) is another concept of Buddhism that was inherited from the traditional Indian religion. In a popular belief form, this teaching has always had moral overtones, as seen in the above story. When this life ends, they teach, one's soul is reborn into another realm and in another form of life. Into what realm and in what life form one is to be reincarnated is dictated by the law of causality, or karma. In the old Buddhist tradition, there are six realms into which one may be reborn, namely, the realms of **inferno, hungry ghosts, beasts, perpetual anger, humans,** and **the heavens.** If you live a life of compassion and kindness, you may be reborn into a higher realm or into a better life within the same realm. On the other hand, if you ignore the pleas of the poor and live a life of greed in this life, you may be born into one of the lower realms, depending on the degree of your greed or evil, and if you are truly evil in this life, you may be reborn into the realm of inferno.

"Past Life Therapy," which is gaining some popularity in the West, assumes this ancient theory of reincarnation and claims that, although we have no conscious memories of our past lives, we still carry some emotional residues of our past lives at a subconscious level, and they often cause us to make inappropriate responses to present experiences.

I have no reason to question the effectiveness of such therapy, but some of our Buddhist friends say that the teaching of *samsara* (reincarnation) is merely an expedient teaching tool with which to guide people to a life of compassion and kindness.[35] Others even question the validity of this teaching because of its seeming contradiction with the original teaching of the Buddha, who rejected the existence of "self *(atman)*" as illusion, while the theory of reincarnation implies that the "self" lives eternally, transmigrating from one life to another.

The idea of "endless transmigration of self" may sound attractive to some of us because it takes the sense of finality out of death. However, most Buddhists think it is a curse, and hope to be freed from the law of *samsara* and karma. They think it is a curse because, no matter how hard we may try to improve our karma in this life, there is no guarantee that we won't be reborn into a miserable life form

---

[35] The idea of "expedient teaching tools" in Buddhism will be discussed more fully later in the section "The Burning House," but the idea has already been briefly discussed earlier in the story of "The Raft."

because we, imperfect beings, may have done some evil things unknowingly. Besides, we never know what we have done in our past lives. That is why many Buddhists, particularly of the Pure Land School, seek to be reborn into the Pure Land with the help of the compassionate Amida Buddha, for the Pure Land is believed to be the final place where there will be no further reincarnations and, thus, no more evil consequences of the karma of your present and past lives.

The Millionaire Peasant

$\mathcal{M}$okichi was an honest and hardworking peasant, but he somehow managed to stay poor. He lived with his wife, Suzu, and his daughter, Tama, in the Province of Suo in western Japan. Mokichi was not quite sixty yet, but years of hard work out in the rice paddies made him look older than he actually was. Suzu was about ten years younger than he, and her beautiful dark hair was still smooth like fine silk. The villagers often commented that her hair should have grown on the head of a princess or a noble lady, not on a poor peasant's wife. Their daughter, Tama, was not only the prettiest girl in the village, but also the most loving daughter one could ever wish for. Despite their poverty, they were a happy family together.

When Tama had just turned seventeen, she was suddenly taken ill. An old village doctor came to see her and said to Mokichi and Suzu:

"Your daughter has a very rare disease. I am afraid no doctor in this country can help her." Then, after a few pensive moments, he said, "I have heard of a German physician called Dr. Siebold in Nagasaki. He is supposed to be one of the best in Europe, and he might know something about it."

Early next morning, Mokichi put his little angel on a small fishing boat and set out on a two day trek to Nagasaki.

Dr. Siebold examined her and told Mokichi, "I am afraid your daughter's illness is terminal, and there is no known cure for it. There is a new drug in Holland that might help slow the progress. It is expensive, but if you are interested, I can have it shipped to you." Mokichi asked him to order the medicine and went home with Tama.

Mokichi worked very hard to pay for Tama's medicine, while Suzu nursed her at home day and night. In spite of their loving care, Tama died before the end of the year. Her death devastated Mokichi. He aged rapidly, got sick often, and could not work anymore. The poor couple had to sell all they had to pay off their debts. Soon, clad in rags, the old man and his wife were begging by a roadside.

"We have worked hard all our lives, and yet we are so poor. *Shikata ga nai* (It can't be helped), it's our karma," said Suzu.

"A bad karma is the only explanation. But if so, there is nothing we can do," said the husband, and took a deep sigh.

"We may not be able to change our past karma, but we can improve our karma for our next life," said Suzu.

"How are we going to do that? We have nothing to give to the monks or to the poor. In fact, there is no one poorer than we."

"I can sell my hair to a wigmaker. I am sure we can make some money, at least enough to feed a few monks in the monastery up in the mountain."

"Your hair is the only treasure you have. Don't do it," said Mokichi.

That very day, however, Suzu cut her silky dark hair and sold it to a wigmaker. With the money she got, she bought a sack of rice. She then went into the forest behind the village and picked a basketful of mushrooms. She cooked the rice and took it to the monastery with a mushroom dish.

"Thank you, Suzu, for your gift. We have more than a hundred monks in this monastery. Whenever we have a donation like this, we all gather in the refectory and partake of it together," said the head priest.

"More than a hundred monks? I only have enough for three or four of your monks," said the woman.

"We'll see," said the priest.

When she looked up and saw all those monks forming a line, each holding a bowl in his hands, she said to herself, "They are going to get mad at me for bringing so little. What do I do?"

Not knowing what to do, Suzu filled the first monk's bowl, then the second, the third, and the fourth. When she saw her pot empty after the fourth monk, she began to pity herself and sob.

"What is the matter? Why are you crying?" asked the next monk in line.

"I have no more rice for you. Please forgive me," she said.

"What do you mean? Your pot is full," said the monk.

Suzu looked at the pot, and it was indeed filled with shiny white rice.

Dumfounded, confused and relieved all at once, she kept serving a bowlful of rice to each monk, and her pot was full each time it was emptied.

Now, among the monks were a few merchants who had survived a shipwreck in the recent typhoon. Having lost the ship and all their belongings, they were staying in the monastery while they were waiting for another ship to come fetch them. They, too, ate Suzu's rice, and they were deeply moved by the story of her generosity.

Weeks later, each of the merchants sent Suzu a third of his wealth in gold, silver and precious jewels. Suzu and Mokichi suddenly became the wealthiest couple in the Province, and, of course, the most generous.

ళ్ళాళ్ళాళ్ళాళ్ళాళ్ళ

The story was originally told over two thousand years ago in India. Its setting was Jeta Grove, where Gotama the Buddha had his first temple. A poor woman in the nearby village sold her hair and fed three thousand disciples of the Buddha. Despite her extreme poverty, her sincere effort to improve her karma for her next life was rewarded with an immediate miracle. I simply recast the story into the early nineteenth century Japan.

In the Hebrew Bible, there is a story of a widow who reminds us of Suzu. She lived in the town of Zarephath when the great famine hit the entire area. Prophet Elijah came to town and met this poor widow. He asked her to bring him some water and a morsel of bread. She said, "I have no bread, but I have a handful of meal in a jar and a little oil in a jug at home. I was going to prepare a meal for my son and myself so that we may eat before we die." Elijah said to her, "Go home and do as you said, but first make me a little cake. God says, 'Your jar will not be emptied and your jug of oil will not fail until our good Lord sends rain on the earth.'" The woman did as Elijah said. "The jar of meal was not emptied, neither did the jug of oil fail, according to the word of God spoken by Elijah" (II Kings 17:16).

Another story is that of the feeding of the multitudes as found in the Gospel of John. Jesus went up the mountain and a huge crowd followed him. After he had preached, he told the disciples to feed them. They all knew it was not possible to feed five thousand people, but a little boy told one of the disciples that he was willing to share his five loaves of barley bread and two fish. Jesus received the boy's offering and told everyone to sit down. Then he took the loaves, and when he had given thanks, he distributed them to those who were there; so also the fish, as much as they wanted. When they were satisfied, he told the disciples, "Gather up the fragments left over, so that nothing may be lost." So they gathered them up, and from the fragments of the five barley loaves, left by those who had eaten, they filled twelve baskets. (John 6:1-14)

In all these stories, a poor and powerless person's gift is miraculously multiplied and serves a greater purpose. The resource of the poor is often more abundant than we can imagine, and the power of the weak is often mightier than that of the powerful.

The Immortal

$\mathcal{W}$hen the Tang Dynasty (618-907 CE) ruled China, Luoyang was the most populous and prosperous city in the whole country. There in the city of Luoyang lived a young homeless man by the name of Zichun Du. He was once a bright, well-mannered young man, but after the passing of his parents, he was no longer the same person. Some say he lost his will to live, and others say he lost his mind.

It was almost the end of autumn; trees had shed most of their leaves, and red persimmons were barely hanging on to the leafless branches. The air was beginning to feel a bit chilly on the cheeks. Zichun was sitting under the West Gate of the city, aimlessly watching people come and go. He had a little basket in front of him just in case someone wanted to drop some money into it, but no one ever did. Unbeknownst to him, across the busy street was an old man in a shabby robe watching Zichun. The old man's long white hair was trailing in the wind.

"What is wrong, son? Why such a sad look on your face?" asked the old man.

"I was wondering where I might sleep tonight. It is getting cold and I have no place to go home to," said the young man.

"O poor fellow. Listen carefully, young man. Wait until the sun casts long shadows. Stand right here and mark the spot on the ground where the head of your shadow will fall. Come back after dark and dig the spot you marked. You will find there a wagon full of gold."

Zichun was skeptical, but in the absence of anything better to do, he did as he was told. Lo and behold, when he dug the ground, he found a wagon full of gold. It made him the richest man in the city overnight, literally. He moved into the biggest and most beautiful mansion in Luoyang and made friends with the most influential and most beautiful people in the city. He hosted a lavish banquet every night, and his friends were always there to enjoy his company. Three years passed and all his money was gone, and the young man was poor and homeless again. As the money was gone, so were his friends. They would not even say hello to him when they saw him on the street.

It was almost the end of autumn again; the air was beginning to feel a bit cold on the cheeks. Zichun was sitting under the West Gate of the city, aimlessly watching people come and go. His basket was empty, just as it was three years ago. The old man was there again, watching him. He slowly walked over to the young man.

"What is wrong, son? Why such a sad look on your face?" asked the old man again.

"I was wondering where I might sleep tonight. It is getting cold and I have no place to go home to," said the young man.

"O poor fellow. You lost your money so soon? Listen carefully. Wait until the sun casts long shadows. Stand right here and mark the spot on the ground where the chest of your shadow will fall. Come back after dark and dig. You will find a wagon full of gold."

Zichun did as the old man told him and found a wagon full of gold again. Once again, he was the richest man in the whole city. He moved into the largest and most beautiful mansion in the city. All his old friends came back to his banquet every night. They all enjoyed his company. Three years went by quickly, and again, all his money was gone. All his friends were gone also. They wouldn't even say hello to him on the street.

One late autumn day, when most of the trees had dropped their leaves and the air was beginning to feel a bit chilly on the cheeks again, Zichun was sitting by the West Gate, aimlessly watching people come and go. There came the same old man, clad in the same shabby robe and his long white hair trailing in the wind.

"What is wrong, son? Why such a sad countenance?" asked the old man.

Zichun looked up and saw the old man, but remained silent.

"You lost your money so soon, son? Do not worry. I can help you again. Wait until the sun casts long shadows…"

"I don't want any money," the young man interrupted. "I am not sad because I have no place to sleep tonight, but because I have lost faith in the human race. When I was rich, they visited me every day as if they were my best friends, but the moment I became poor, nobody cared about a loser like me; they wouldn't even look at me on the street. But I cannot blame them. I was the foolish one. In fact, I am disgusted at myself. I was blinded by the money you let me have, and I blew the opportunity to make something of myself, not just once, but twice." Zichun kept talking. "I know who you are. You are a Taoist adept, one of the Immortals from the Mystic Isles. You made me the richest man in the city with your supernatural power twice, and I am now sick of being rich; I hate humanity. Make me an immortal like you, so that I can transcend the stupidity and ugliness of humankind. Teach me and train me. I will do anything," implored Zichun.

"Indeed, my name is Li Tie-Guai, one of the Immortals of the Mystic Isles. When I saw you first, I thought you might be a good candidate for immortality. That's why I helped you in the first place, and I have not given up on you yet. I will help you again and train you to achieve immortality. The training will be hard, but you can make it. Come with me to Mt. Emei," said the old man. They mounted on the old man's bamboo stick and flew to Mt. Emei.

When they arrived at his mountain cave, the Immortal said to the young man, "Excuse me for a while, I have a little business to attend to in heaven. I will be back soon enough, but you must promise me never to say a word to anyone while I am gone. Otherwise, your quest for transcendence and immortality will end the moment you have uttered a word."

"I promise not to say a word to anyone while you are gone," said the young man.

Soon after the old man had left, a ferocious tiger appeared crouching before him and roared the scariest roar he had ever heard. Behind him was a large serpent preparing to devour him. When the tiger and the serpent jumped up to attack him, he almost screamed, but he kept his mouth shut as he had promised. Fortunately, they were mere apparitions; they disappeared like morning mist before they reached him. Earthquakes, hails, thunder and lightning threatened him all night long, but he did not open his mouth. Just before the dawn, a fierce looking warrior came up to him and said, "What are you doing in my mountain? What is your name?" Zichun remained silent. "Speak! Otherwise, I will kill you." When he saw Zichun determined not to open his mouth, the angry warrior pierced Zichun's chest with his spear with one quick thrust.

With that thrust, Zichun fell through the crack of the rock all the way down to the underworld, where he was forced to stand before the throne of King Yama, the Ruler of the Underworld. In a thunderous voice, the King said, "Speak now! What is your name? Why are you here?" Though trembling with fear, the young man did not open his mouth. It made the king furious, and he ordered his servant devils to torture him, but Zichun kept his mouth shut through the ordeal. The devils then brought out two skinny donkeys before him. They were not in human forms, but Zichun immediately knew that they were his parents. The devils began to beat them with nail-studded clubs. After a few minutes of beating, one of the donkeys collapsed. Bleeding and gasping for air, it said to him, "Zichun, I am your mother. Do not worry about us. If you do not want to say anything to Yama the King, do not say anything. That's all right with us. We love you just the same. The only thing we want is your happiness, Zichun." With tears in his eyes, he ran to his mother, picked her up in his arms, and said, "Mother!"

The moment he uttered the word, he was right back at the West Gate, standing with the Immortal. Strangely, however, there was a sign of new life on his pale face.

"You know you can no longer be immortal," said the old man.

"I know. How could I have remained silent when my own mother was being beaten like that? I could not become immortal at the expense of my own mother. If I did, I would be regretting it the rest of my immortal life," said the young man. The tears began to run down his face again.

"To tell you the truth, I was going to have the devils finish you off if you did not say anything to your mother at that time. If you could not even be human, how could you be one of us? You are now sick of being rich, sick of humanity; you have failed to be immortal. What would you do now, son?" asked the old man.

"I am going to live as a human being as honestly as I can. That's all I want. Being human is not so bad after all."

రెరెరెరెరెరెరె

Despite Zichun's disappointment in the dark side of humanity, the story ends with an affirmation of humanity. We are so selfish that even our friendship is often based on mutual usefulness, self-interest, and convenience, and not on love or loyalty. Zichun wanted to transcend all those flaws and limitations of humanity by becoming one of the Immortals, but his mother's selfless love and sacrifice made him realize that humanity could be much more than the selfishness and opportunism of the people he knew.

My rendition of the story is based on a short story *To Shishun*[36] (Zichun Du) by Ryonosuke Akutagawa, arguably the most brilliant Japanese writer of the early twentieth century. Akutagawa based his story on the ninth century Chinese Taoist novel, *Life of Zichun Du*.

Despite the metaphysical sophistication of Lau Tzu and Chuang Tzu, Taoism as a popular folk religion has absorbed and produced many superstitions, supernatural fantasies, and magic portions for eternal youth and immortality. Despite their implausible promises, they reveal our hidden desire for transcending life's limitations. After all, who has not wished, one time or another, to rise above life's petty concerns and pains or to defy aging and enjoy eternal youth? The Zichun Du story, however, tells us that ultimately we must be able to accept our own humanity, its bright and dark sides together, its noble and ignoble sides together, and live as a whole person as honestly and truthfully as possible.

My first encounter with this story took place in my high school freshman year, when the school's drama club selected it for the year's performance. A friend of mine got a part in the play and told me about it. I was so intrigued by the story that I volunteered to help paint the backdrops for the play. When I read the script, I immediately identified myself with Zichun's character, as I was also a quiet, awkward, sensitive and idealistic teenager. Like Zichun, I had lost my mother, too. Many would readily betray you or leave you whenever it is more convenient to do so, but there

---

[36] Akutagawa, Ryunosuke, *Akutagawa RyunosukeZenshu Vol. 2* (Chikuma Shobo, Tokyo, 1957) p. 244

is always someone, like Zichun's mother, who loves you, no matter what, in spite of all your imperfections and flaws. Do not give up on humanity; give it another chance. That was what I read in the story.

The Immortal's suggestion that the gold was to be found where Zichun's shadow would fall was symbolic of the Taoist philosophy of Yin and Yang. The small white dot (eye) in the dark side of the symbol indicates a new hope emerging out of the shadow. The dot is "a wagon full of gold" in the Zichun Du story. The shadow is actually intertwined with the bright side anyway and they are part of each other.

Learn to love humanity despite all its flaws and limitations. Human beings can indeed be selfish, cruel, and unfaithful, but they can also be self-giving, compassionate, and truthful. We must be able to embrace our humanity in its entirety, both the shadow and the light together, both Yin and Yang together. Our healing will begin when we are able to embrace both Yin and Yang. To become a whole person, accept and embrace your femininity and masculinity, your introversion and extroversion, your insecurity and security, your weaknesses and strengths, and all other aspects of your life that are opposing, yet complementing. To become a whole society, embrace all the opposing elements as they are indeed complementary—majority and minority, male and female, gay and straight, etc., etc.

As Carl Jung suggests, integrating one's shadow is the beginning of one's healing. God has accepted us all for what we are, and still loves us. Ultimately, it is not a matter of "either-or" choices, but of "both-and" integration that makes us stronger and healthier both personally and collectively.

The Burning House

On a certain town in a certain country, a very wealthy wise man lived with his many children. He had a large house with just one door. One day, a fire broke out in the house and the flames began to spread quickly. His children were trapped inside the burning house. The man shouted at his children, "Fire! Fire! Get out of the house at once!" But the children were all engrossed in the games they were playing and did not heed his warning. The father, remembering that the children liked playing with toy carts, thought of a practical way to lure them out of the burning house. He called out to them, "Listen! Outside the door are carts that you have always wanted: a cart pulled by goats, a cart pulled by deer, and a cart pulled by oxen. Why don't you come out and play with them?" The father knew that these things would get his children's immediate attention. As soon as they heard it, the children rushed out of the burning house, and they were saved in the nick of time. Outside, however, the father did not have the carts he had promised. Instead, he had a better cart draped with precious stones and pulled by white bullocks. The father did not deliver what he had promised, but the important thing was that the children were rescued from the house on fire. Not only that, they have now received the greatest vehicle, which can lead them to eternal salvation.

కికికికికికి

The parable is found in the Saddharma Pundarika Sutra, commonly known as the Lotus Sutra, upon which

Nichiren sects of Buddhism were founded. The parable was set as part of a dialogue between the Buddha and his disciple Shariputra, but the sutra itself was written much later, probably in the first century in Kashmir. The sutra's original intention for the parable was to teach readers that the Buddha was trying to rescue all sentient beings trapped in the world aflame with passion for momentary pleasures by means of enticement. The toys he promised may not have been absolute truth, but a means of compassion, nevertheless. The father lured his children out of danger by promising goat, deer and ox carts, but his plan, aside from saving them from the impending danger, was to give them a much better one, "a cart draped with precious stones and pulled by white bullocks," namely a vehicle of nirvana. Buddhists freely admit that not all their teachings are ultimate truths in themselves, but practical and expedient means by which to guide people to enlightenment. In other words, they do not intend some of their teachings to be absolute or final, but encourage followers to go beyond them to a far greater truth. This is another example of what we discussed earlier in the story of The Raft in the swift river.

The biblical parables of Jesus (*parabolé* in Greek) and the Buddhist parables (*paryâyas* in Sanskrit) are very similar in many respects. In fact, some scholars suggest that they were more closely related in their development than previously believed. Whether in the Bible or in the Buddhist texts, most parables were meant to stir the readers' imaginations and encourage them to think outside the box. Those who heard Jesus' parables were left puzzled at first as they were designed not to be understood readily. Besides, there are so many layers of meaning that different people take away different things at different times, depending on the reader's life experience and circumstance. Just like the parables of Jesus, Buddhist parables are also puzzling and have many layers of meanings.

Like the children in the parable, we are blinded by our pursuit of the momentary pleasures of life (illusions of fulfillment) and are neither seeing the danger of this way of life nor seeking more important truths.

Some Buddhist leaders have used the Parable of the Burning House as a way to help substance abusers out of their addictive habits. Others have seen the burning house as a metaphor for abusive domestic relationships, and used the story to help them out of their codependency. Whatever one sees in the parable, it challenges those who feel trapped in their circumstances to see the imminent danger in where they are and to get out of it. The parable conveys a sense of urgency, which helps in many such instances.

ॐॐॐॐॐॐॐ

A more pertinent message of the parable for most of us, however, may have to do with our pursuit of materialistic values, such as seen in advertisements on TV and magazines. Because of the constant reinforcement of such values, it has become rather difficult to resist them. We do not all have to look like movie stars or fashion models. We do not even have to have the latest models of automobiles or electronic gadgets. When we are trapped in the world burning with the fire of materialistic pursuit, of consumerism and competition, we may not be able to heed a call for spiritual values, such as love, faith, compassion, peace and justice. Like the desperate father in the parable of the burning house, we might have to resort to more practical and expedient ways to redirect people's attention to the more urgent and important issues of spiritual values.

ॐॐॐॐॐॐॐ

Jesus also warned against our habitual pursuit of material values, and he called us to seek higher and more spiritual values, which he called "a treasure in heaven."

Let us hear what Jesus had to say about it in Luke 12:22-32:

"Therefore I tell you, do not worry about your life, what you will eat, or about your body, what you will wear. For life is more than food, and the body more than clothing... Consider the lilies, how they grow: they neither toil nor spin; yet I tell you, even Solomon in all his glory was not clothed like one of these. But if God so clothes the grass of the field, which is alive today and tomorrow is thrown into the oven, how much more will God clothe you—you of little faith! And do not keep striving for what you are to eat and what you are to drink, and do not keep worrying. For it is the nations of the world that strive after all these things, and your God knows that you need them. Instead, strive for the kingdom of God, and these things will be given to you as well.... Sell possessions and give alms. Make purses for yourselves that do not wear out, an unfailing treasure in heaven, where no thief comes near and no moth destroys."

The Hidden Treasure

$\mathcal{T}$he world's largest Buddha made entirely of pure gold is housed in a modest Buddhist temple in the busy Chinatown district of Bangkok, Thailand. The temple is called Wat Traimit. This fifteen foot high statue is made of pure gold, weighing five and a half tons. Based on the style of art, historians have determined that the statue was made in the mid-thirteenth century during the reign of the Sukhothai Dynasty. Aside from its artistic and religious value, the gold alone is worth almost one billion dollars in today's gold market. Yet, much of its seven hundred year history is shrouded in mystery. We don't know who commissioned it, who the artist was, or why and under what circumstances it was made. All we know is that it was covered with plaster and nobody knew that under the clay crust was a majestic gold image of the Buddha until 1957.

Such a magnificent statue must have been considered a national treasure and placed in a grand sanctuary of one of the greatest temples of the nation, but we don't know where it was. During the Sukhothai period, Thailand was repeatedly attacked by adjacent Burma. During those assaults, many temples and royal monuments were destroyed, sacred manuscripts were burned, and anything made of precious metal was seized and taken to Burma. When an imminent Burmese invasion was rumored, the priests of the temple must have covered the statue with plaster to conceal it and protect it from pillaging. Their strategy worked and the statue survived the enemy's savage onslaught, but none of the priests survived to tell their posterity that the clay image of the Buddha was actually solid gold. The Burmese army had since been driven out of Thai territory and dynasties had come and gone, but the golden Buddha remained hidden under the clay crust.

There is no record of where the statue had been until the mid-nineteenth century, when King Rama III, whose policy it was to revitalize the nation under Buddhism, built a number of new temples in Bangkok. Wat Phrayakrai was one of the temples he built, and the clay statue was installed there as its principal Buddha image. The temple did not last very long, however. It was closed in 1931. Later that year, the East Asiatic Company, a Copenhagen-based steamship company, acquired the land where the temple stood. The temple had been closed, but those involved felt that a new home must be found soon for the sacred objects left in the abandoned temple. With the help of the Bangkok Ecclesiastical Commission, an arrangement was made to relocate the clay image to the Wat Traimit Temple in Bangkok, but the temple did not have a proper room to keep it.

In 1957, twenty years later, the construction of a new Buddha hall for the clay Buddha was finished. When the workers hoisted it with a crane, an unthinkable accident happened — the statue lost balance and crashed to the ground. The Abbot Phra Visutha-thibordee and others rushed to the scene to assess the damage. They found a crack on the image, but it appeared repairable. The moment they heaved a sigh of relief, the Abbot saw through the crack a golden gleam. The workers carefully removed the crust until a magnificent golden Buddha emerged. It was the most elegant and most precious image of the Buddha they had ever seen.

Today, the golden Buddha is enshrined prominently in the stately Buddha Hall of Wat Traimit, and a piece of the clay crust is also on display. The treasure that was covered up in obscurity for hundreds of years is now shown in its full glory.

In the New Testament Gospels there are a few stories of hidden treasure. One of them is found in Matthew 13:

"The kingdom of heaven is like treasure hidden in a field, which someone found and hid; then in his joy he goes and sells all that he has and buys that field."
(Matthew 13:44)

This parable is about an unexpected discovery of the hidden treasure. The person who uncovered the treasure was obviously a tenant worker who did not even own the land. Day after day, he went to work in the field with no great joy, but when he discovered the treasure, "in his joy" he covered it up, went home, and sold everything he had in order to buy the land that contained the treasure in it. To me, the field he worked day after day is a metaphor for our lives. It is not particularly remarkable, but when the treasure is found in it, it suddenly becomes more precious than all his possessions.

Accepting and embracing both the dirt and treasure is a result of discovering a new self, which is a true treasure. The "new self" is that which is a manifestation of the kingdom reality or of eternal bliss, and owes to the world nothing but love. That is so valuable that it cannot be replaced by anything else you possess.

Through my ministry with recovering alcoholics and drug addicts, I have come to learn that the number one cause of addiction is poor self-esteem. To recover from addiction, they need to discover themselves and realize that they have a golden treasure inside. The treasure is everywhere waiting to be uncovered. The Gospel of Thomas says, "The kingdom of the father is spread upon the earth, and people do not see it" (Saying #113). Do we know we have treasure inside? Do we know that we have the kingdom reality hidden inside? Do we know it is worth more than all our material possessions put together? If we do, then we will know that we can accept ourselves, including our dark side.

Chapter Six:

Old, New Values

牧牛 五

"Finally, beloved, whatever is true, whatever is honorable, whatever is just, whatever is pure, whatever is pleasing, whatever is commendable, if there is any excellence and if there is anything worthy of praise, think about these things."

— Philippians 4:8

The Golden Deer

$\mathcal{O}$n Varanasi by the Ganges lived a foolish young man. He inherited immense fortune left by his late father, but in a few short years, he squandered all his money on account of his lavish lifestyle; all he had left was a mounting debt. As a result, he had to try to elude his tenacious creditors every day. "This is no life; I would rather be dead," he said to himself, and plunged into the swirling waters where the Ganges bent and narrowed. As soon as he hit the water, he realized what a foolish thing he had done. So, at the top of his voice, he screamed, "Help! I am drowning! Help, somebody!"

In the most peaceful part of the forest, where mango trees grew, lived a magnificent deer. His fur shone like polished gold, his feet were as white as milk, his antlers were like fine silver, his dark eyes glistened like precious jewels, and his posture was regal. When he heard the man's cry for help, the deer ran to the river and jumped in. After a few minutes of struggle, he was able to return safely to the shore with the half-dead man on his back. He took the man to his nest and nursed him back to his old self. When the man was ready to go home, the golden deer asked the man to promise never to tell anyone about where he lived, and the man promised.

In the royal palace, the queen had a strange dream one night. She saw in her dream a beautiful golden deer walking peacefully among trees. The queen told the king about the dream and asked him to find the deer. The king's proclamation went out immediately and was posted all over the kingdom. It read:

"An excellent and beautiful village, where fair
maidens live, has been set aside as a reward
to anyone who guides the king to the place
where a golden deer can be found."

The man who was rescued by the deer a few days earlier saw
the sign. Even though he had promised never to reveal the
golden deer's secret mango grove to anyone, he figured that
showing the king where to find him and claiming the reward
would be the easiest way to become rich again, so he went to
the palace. The king was delighted to meet him, and he had
the young man lead him and his army to the hidden mango
grove by the river.

"There he is." He pointed to the golden deer. The
king ordered his army to surround the area and get the bows
and arrows ready. The deer now knew he was surrounded but
did not seem intimidated by it. Appearing even more
dignified, he approached the king and said to him, "No man
was supposed to know where I lived. Who told you where to
find me, Sire?" The king dismounted his elephant and
pointed to the man behind him and said, "This man told me
where to find you." "I see that the man sold me, who saved
his life." The deer then told the whole story to the king, and
added, "Some humans say one thing to your face but say
something else behind your back. It is sad, but they need
mercy, too." The king grew indignant as he listened. "You,
ungrateful wretch! You shall be beheaded!" shouted the king
angrily to the man.

"My lord, that man indeed betrayed me, but please be
merciful to him. I do not wish his life to be taken on my
account. Ingratitude is a sign of foolishness, and not reacting
to it violently is a sign of wisdom. Please give him the
reward you promised and let him go, but do with me as you
wish," pleaded the deer.

"Your graciousness moved me deeply," said the king.
"You are compassionate to him who does not deserve it, and
courageous and calm in the face of your fate. You must be a

great Bodhisattva. You are a much greater being than humans. I now proclaim that no one in my kingdom shall ever hunt for deer."

Deer and humans lived in peace happily ever after in the kingdom of Varanasi by the Ganges. The deer was indeed a Bodhisattva, and a few cycles of reincarnation later, he became Gotama the Buddha, the Enlightened One. In fact, Gotama preached his first sermon at the place called Mrgadāva (Deer Garden) in Varanasi.

❧❧❧❧❧❧❧

The story is one of more than five hundred stories collected in the Pali literature of Jataka, which is part of the Theravada Canon. The Jataka stories are all about the good deeds done by the Buddha in his past lives. The assumption is that the greatness of the Buddha is a result of a truly great karma accumulated through innumerable cycles of reincarnation. Therefore, the Jataka stories are intended to enforce the belief that a good karmic seed bears good fruits in the next life.

❧❧❧❧❧❧❧

The culture of utilitarian individualism, in which we are immersed, determines the value of each and every thing by its present usefulness to individuals. The story of the Golden Deer reminds us that there is something far more important than usefulness to individuals, namely gratitude — gratitude to those who have made us who we are: our parents, teachers, friends, communities, and even strangers.

The city of Nara, the ancient capital of Japan, is famous for the enormous bronze statue of the Buddha housed in the largest and arguably the most elegant wooden structure in the world, Todaiji Great Buddha Hall, but it is also known for the large population of friendly deer, who greet all persons who come to visit this ancient capital. It is interesting to know that the city is still keeping the promise made between the king of Varnasi and the Golden Deer in the mango grove by the Ganges thousands of years ago, thousands of miles away, as a perpetual reminder of how important it is to remember the debt of gratitude even in the modern culture of secular individualism.

Morning Glory and Tea House

$\mathcal{T}$ea ceremony was unknown in Japan until Zen Master Eisai introduced it as part of monastic Zen training upon his return from China in 1191 CE. The popularity of tea ceremony gradually spread beyond the bounds of monastic life. By the sixteenth century, tea ceremony, as we know it today, was perfected both as an art form and a unique philosophy by a tea master named Sen Rikyu (1521-1591).

When Lord Hideyoshi had finally consolidated all the provincial powers of the nation under his military dictatorship, he appointed Rikyu as his tea master. In those days, morning-glory was still a novelty in Japan. Rikyu planted the seeds in his garden. He carefully guided the vines to climb and twine around the frames he had built. When the time came, it blossomed brilliantly. Hundreds of flowers of assorted colors invigorated the dull air of the sultry mid-summer days of Kyoto. Rumor of his garden's magnificent beauty soon reached Hideyoshi, and the dictator invited himself to view Rikyu's famous morning-glories. A few hours before Hideyoshi's arrival, however, Rikyu went out to the garden and removed all the blossoms and put a single blossom of morning-glory in a vase inside his tea room. Hideyoshi, who expected a garden full of blossoms, was visibly upset, and demanded an explanation. Rikyu said to him, "Sire, I took the trouble of removing all the blossoms but one, because the fragile aesthetic quality of morning-glories cannot be observed if there are many of them." The true value is not in how much you have, but in how much you can appreciate the one you have. Hideyoshi accepted the explanation for the time being, but he knew it was a challenge to his fondness for materialistic extravagance. The love-hate relationship between Hideyoshi and Rikyu intensified around that time. It was not just a conflict between the two strong-willed men, but between the two different sensibilities these two giants represented.

A few years later, when Hideyoshi's luxurious villa, Flying Clouds Pavilion, was completed, he ordered Rikyu to build a tea house in the compounds. As you might suspect, the dictator expected to see a magnificent tea house with lavish use of gold and precious timber, consistent with the rest of the architecture. To Hideyoshi's dismay, however, Rikyu built a small, simple house with a grass-thatched roof, practically a peasant's hut. He wanted to tell Hideyoshi that true richness must be found in the poverty of a rustic shed.

The tea houses Rikyu designed had a very small entrance called *Nijiriguchi* (kneeling entrance). The guests who entered the tea house, no matter how high their ranks were, had to remove their swords, kneel, and bow to clear the low beam of the entrance. Tea houses were Rikyu's sanctuary where all people were considered equal, and even Hideyoshi, the supreme military dictator, had to disarm and kneel. One's rank and prestige outside the tea room are forgotten inside, because the sanctity of human beings does not depend on their status in society.

The ambivalent relationship between these two great men continued to grow in intensity until Hideyoshi finally ordered Rikyu to commit ritual suicide. Upon receiving the order, Rikyu retired to his tea room, quietly enjoyed his last cup of tea and composed the following Chinese poem:

> *Seventy years of life —*
> *Ha ha! and what a fuss!*
> *With this sacred sword of mine,*

Rikyu's aesthetics are often described as that of *wabi* (poverty, insufficiency) and *sabi* (aloneness, tranquility). Between them exists a subtle difference in nuances, but *wabi* and *sabi* are often used together to reinforce each other. They both indicate external poverty with internal richness. In other words, Rikyu's tea ceremony is an art of finding richness in poverty, fullness in aloneness, and perfection in imperfection. His teacups are not perfectly shaped, but those who drink from them experience a perfect harmony with nature. His tea houses are simple, but they are sanctuaries in which one can find the dignity of every person who enters it.

ॐॐॐॐॐॐॐ

Join Patricia Heinicke in her prayer response:

My knees are locked tight.
My sword lies heavily at my side.
I cannot come to tea.

I am not so fully armed that I cannot name my
weapons.
Here are a few:
Judgment. Isolation. Joylessness.
Fear of attack makes me aggressive
and prevents me from making
a gracious acceptance.

Or perhaps mine are defensive weapons?
I protect myself with the rich armor of gifts,
grasped and shaped as if my own creation:
strength, power, generosity,
pride, piety, a nurturing heart.
I clothe myself in their complex shield,

---

[37] Rikyu is quoting the 9th century Zen Master Lin Chi's famous saying, "If you meet the Buddha, kill him; if you meet the Patriarch, kill him."

too heavy for the tea house.

But You disregard this arsenal.
You welcome me, simply me,
into Your presence.
You teach me the etiquette of communion:
a curtsy, warm smile,
"Thank you so much for having me."
Simply me.

Give me the brave courtesy
to acknowledge the invitation I receive
and to stack my weapons quietly
outside the door.
Perhaps after tea
I might wear them more lightly.

— Patricia Heinicke, Jr.

Spider's Thread

*G*otama the Buddha was taking a leisurely walk in the Pure Land one crisp morning. He deeply inhaled the air filled with the sweet aroma of lotus flowers. A few steps away was a pond where the beautiful white lotus flowers released their fragrance. As he looked down between the flowers and through the crystal clear waters, he caught a sight of the Purgatory way down below, where thousands of sinners were being tormented in the pond of blood and on the hills of needles. He recognized among those suffering sinners a face he remembered well. It was that of Kandata, the notorious thief. He did evil things all his life, but the Buddha remembered one incident: when Kandata was walking through a forest, he found a tiny spider walking awkwardly across his path. When he was about to step on it, he said to himself: "Wait. Even a little creature like this has life. There is no reason to destroy it." So he did not squash the little creature. Afraid that someone else might step on it, he picked it up and gently put it on a little branch of a roadside shrub. From that little incident, the Buddha knew that Kandata had a warm heart in spite of all the wicked things he had done.

The Buddha felt compassion for Kandata and wished to save him from the agony of the Purgatory for one good deed he had performed. The Buddha found a spider on a lotus leaf, put it on the palm of his hand and let it spin a shiny thread. It went down deeper and deeper until it reached the Purgatory.

It was pitch dark and eerily quiet in spite of the thousands of sinners struggling to stay afloat in the pond of blood. From there, Kandata looked up in desperation and saw a silvery thread coming down directly toward him from the bright spot high above. He knew that the bright spot was the only opening into the Pure Land. Thinking, therefore, that the thread may possibly be his way out of this hellish existence and into the Pure Land, he grabbed the thread and began to climb up. He was almost out of the mouth of the Purgatory. The thought of leaving the agony behind and moving to the blissful peace of the Pure Land entered his mind and made his heart glad at last. To give one last look at the place where he was tormented for so long, he looked down. He saw many others climbing the thread behind him, like ants after a sugar cake. He thought their weight might break the fragile thread and he, along with many others, would fall right back where they came from, so he shouted, "Get off my thread! This is mine! Get off!" At that very moment, the spider's thread broke just above Kandata, and all fell down back into the Purgatory. The Buddha's heart grew sad, for he wished to save all of them. Such was the Buddha's Compassion! Such was Kandata's selfishness!

ॐॐॐॐॐॐॐ

This is the gist of the story written by a Japanese novelist, Ryunosuke Akutagawa,[38] in 1918. It has since been quoted in many Buddhist sermons and essays. The story, however, is a Buddhist version of the Russian fable "An Onion," which Akutagawa found in Fyodor Dostoyevsky's *The Brothers Karamazov*.[39] He transferred it to a Buddhist context and rewrote it in the style of classic Indian literature. Be that as it may, what Akutagawa tried to show was the self-destructiveness of humanity's selfishness in contrast to the unconditional and indiscriminate compassion of the divine. By trying to save his life, and his life alone, Kandata

---

[38] Akutagawa, Ryunosuke, *Akutagawa Ryunosuke Zenshu Vol. 1* (Chikuma Shobo, Tokyo, 1958, p. 262)
[39] It is in the Book VII, Chapter 3 of *The Brothers Karamazov*

lost his, while the Buddha's desire was to save all the suffering beings in spite of their evil past.

Jesus said, "Those who want to save their life will lose it, and those who lose their life for my sake, and for the sake of the gospel, will save it" (Mark 8:35). If saving our own life becomes our primary concern, our life will lose its meaning. If, on the other hand, we are willing to give our life to something and someone other than ourselves, we will gain it. To lose one's life for Christ and for his Gospel means to gain the meaning of life by finding a purpose bigger than our petty concerns for self-preservation. Gotama the Buddha taught that Renunciation and Compassion constitute salvation. In our society today, we have become so preoccupied with the pursuit and protection of our own individualistic happiness that our life is beginning to lose its meaning and purpose. The irony of our society is that our individualism has come to the point where it cannot even fulfill individuals' needs, for the greatest need of individuals is to be in a loving and caring relationship. The time has come for us to look at the way of Love and Compassion again lest we should repeat Kandata's tragedy.

The One-Eyed Dragon

$\mathcal{A}$ young artist was commissioned to paint a picture of a dragon on the ceiling of a well-known Buddhist temple in China. Knowing that hundreds of people would be viewing the mural every day for ages to come, the ambitious artist poured his heart and soul into the painting. The priests and patrons, who had come to see the progress of his work, were all astonished by the remarkable life-likeness of the mystical creature. It was indeed a great piece of art, unmatched in its power and majestic beauty. When the scaffold had been removed and the Hall cleansed to make ready for a service of consecration, the artist noticed that the dragon in the picture was missing one of its eyes. Pressured to finish the work in time for the service, the artist had forgotten to paint the second eye. But there was no time to erect the scaffold again. So he soaked his brush in the paint, stood directly underneath the dragon and took aim at the spot where the eye was supposed to be. After taking a big breath, he hurled the brush toward the ceiling with all his strength. It hit the target right in the middle, and the picture was now complete.

The moment the eye was painted in, however, the dragon suddenly began to move its powerful tail. Dark clouds gathered in the sky and lightning struck. With a long and thunderous roar, the creature soared high above the temple and ascended straight into heaven. When quietness returned to the temple, the ceiling was completely bare. Weeks later, the artist painted a dragon again, but deliberately left one of its eyes unfinished. Thus, the temple, known as the Heavenly Dragon Temple, is famous for its magnificent mural of a one-eyed dragon.

꺄꺄꺄꺄꺄꺄꺄

We live in a fast-paced, pressure-filled world. We always seem to be in a hurry to meet the deadline for one thing or another. In fact, we are so busy all the time that we only have time to deal with the urgent, and not enough time to do the important.

When I lived in Japan, I used to enjoy traveling by train because it gave me a chance to appreciate the beautiful countryside. In those days, the train was pulled by old-fashioned, coal-burning locomotives. I would board the train after supper at Osaka Station and sleep through the night until the rays of the morning sun gently hit my eyes. Between meals, I would constantly look out the window to admire the breathtaking view of the coastline and the brilliant foliage of the mountains, and finally arrive in Tokyo in mid-afternoon. It took me 18 hours to travel from Osaka to Tokyo. Whenever I visit Japan now, I usually take the "bullet train." It only takes three hours to travel the same distance. Houses and fields, rivers and bridges fly by the window so fast that my eyes can't even follow them. It makes me wonder how many lonely souls I pass each and every minute of the ride. We may marvel at the technology that has enabled such an efficient means of ground transportation, but how good is the technology if we can't even stop to savor the beauty of the land or comfort the lonely souls along the way? The efficient, high-technological civilization is indeed magnificent, but we must remember not to leave its eyes unpainted.

Among Japanese Buddhists is a long cherished tradition of paying homage to the "Forty-Eight Buddhist Sites of Western Japan." Clad in white traveling clothes and chanting a sutra along the way, pilgrims walk in slow and deliberate strides. Their goal is to visit all forty-eight holy places, but you would never see a pilgrim drive a vehicle or run from one holy place to another because they all know that each step of their journey is as holy as their destinations. Whenever they meet another person along the way, they stop and put their palms together in a posture of worship. I wish all of us could adopt this beautiful custom so that we, too, may learn to take time and put our palms together to recognize the holy in every person we meet in our journey of life.

Slow down, world! Our picture is not finished yet. Give us time to paint the other eye, through which we will behold the wonders of God's marvelous creation and recognize the inner sanctuary of every soul. Then, only then, our civilization might come to life and soar to its new height.

The Blank Sutras

*I*n *The Journey to the West* is another interesting episode. After their long and dangerous westward journey, Hsüan-tsang and his company finally arrived in India and obtained a set of new sacred scriptures. On their way home to China, a strong wind arose one day and blew all the scriptures away. As they were trying to fetch the scattered paper, they realized that the pages were blank. Hsüan-tsang was greatly disappointed. After all, he did not risk his life to come all the way to India for blank sutras. Suddenly, the Buddha appeared before the disappointed priest and said, "Those blank sutras were actually far more sacred and far superior to the sutras that are filled with words, but if you desire them, I can give these to you." The Buddha then handed him a new set of sutras, which he spent the rest of his life translating into Chinese.

To be historically accurate, Hsüan-tsang actually stayed in India for a few years to study Sanskrit and the new Mahayana philosophy of Asanga and Vasubandhu under the most learned scholars of his time. He personally selected the Sanskrit texts he wanted to take home and translate. He was a linguist; he would not have chosen blank books. Be that as it may, the Buddha's words in this story reveal a profound truth: "Those blank sutras I gave you earlier were far more sacred and far superior to the sutras that are filled with words." Truth lies not in words, but between them and beyond them. Truth begins where words cease. We must learn to listen to the Great Silence that transcends words and yet contains them all. That's what the Buddha was trying to tell Hsüan-tsang.

Ryōanji Temple in Kyoto is known for its exquisite meditation garden. Fifteen rocks are arranged beautifully on a bed of white sand. At first, your eyes are focused on the rocks and how they are arranged. After a while, however, your eyes shift to the space between the rocks. You then realize that it is the blank space that gives this garden its aesthetic and spiritual qualities. Buddhists may call this blank space "Emptiness" or "Nothingness." Others might call it a field of spirituality. It is like the blank sutras that Hsüan-tsang first received, but lost. No matter what we call it, it is true that many of us know only very little of it because we pay too much attention to what is visible and not enough to what is invisible.

The relationship between the rocks and the empty space in the Ryōanji garden may be likened to the relationship between consciousness and unconsciousness. It is well known that the Swiss psychologist C. G. Jung explored the unconscious level of human psyche through the study of myths, symbols and dreams and advocated the importance of integrating the unconscious with the conscious. He writes, "Consciousness, no matter how extensive it may be, must always remain the smaller circle within the greater circle of the unconscious, an island surrounded by the sea; and like the sea itself, the unconscious yields an endless and self-replenishing abundance of living creatures, a wealth beyond our fathoming."[40] Buddhists, particularly of Zen schools, have always been aware of the wisdom of the unconscious and tried to tap into its abundant resource through meditation and emptying of conscious minds. The Western theology, on the other hand, has been trying to deal with the mystery of God at the conscious level through words and logic. Hence, in my estimate, the Western methods have not been as effective in penetrating the unconscious level of our minds. Here lies

---

[40] Jung, C.G., "The Practice of Psychology," *The Collected Works of C.G. Jung* (Pantheon Books, New York, 1958) 16, par. 366

another area where the Western and the Eastern practices can complement each other for the further development of human spirituality.

❧❧❧❧❧❧❧

I know I have written many words in these pages, but I also know that the true journey begins when words cease and the Spirit takes over. Words can be a great guide in the beginning, but we must go beyond words to journey into the mystery of God's presence in life. Lao Tzu wrote in his *Tao Te Ching*, "One who knows speaks not; one who speaks knows not." We must stop being so noisy so that we may hear the silent voice of the spirit within. We must stop being so talkative so that we may become aware of God's ineffable grace that embraces our entire being.

We entitled this humble book of stories *On the Back of a Buffalo - Eastern Stories for Western Journey - Interfaith Dialogue*. On the back of a buffalo, we have ventured out to the East in search of a buffalo. Through these stories, we have taken a glimpse of Eastern spirituality. We now invite you to come home to your own faith, hopefully with a new perspective. I hope you are more receptive to what your own religious tradition has been trying to say, because your spirituality has been widened and enriched by these stories.

Throughout this book our buffalo has assumed many names—ox, mighty dragon, Holy Spirit, *Buddhata*, great emptiness, blank space, eternal grace, and life-nurturing force within. The same buffalo will now carry you home to the bliss of peace and harmony. Now it is time to open the pages of the blank sutras, which the readers must translate into the language of their own faith.

Epilogue

Those who have read this far may be wondering whether the author still considers himself Christian and, if so, why. Given the mostly positive views on the Eastern, particularly Buddhist, philosophies shared in this book, those questions are to be expected. As a matter of fact, I have wondered about them myself. I believe the readers are entitled to some explanations.

My answer to the first question is easily "Yes." Despite my obvious affinity with the Eastern and Buddhist philosophy, I do believe in God of Christ. The ongoing dialogue I have with the Bible still inspires me to keep returning to the grace of God in Christ, and I am still committed to the mission and ministry of the church. To answer the question on why, however, I need to say a little more about my background.

I have always been Christian as far back as I can remember. My mother died when I was six, and my eldest sister followed her only a couple of years later. My sister was only eighteen when she succumbed to leukemia. As the youngest in the family, the subsequent arrival of a stepmother and the ensuing years of chaos and conflict at home were almost unbearable, but I knew God's spirit was at work. It was the grace of God and the church's ministry that sustained me and kept me from falling apart. My other sister was my Sunday school teacher. I still remember the warmth and firmness of her hand that held mine as we walked to church together every Sunday. She wanted to make sure that I had some positive experience of God's loving care in the formative years of my life, and the warmth of her hand was tangible evidence of God's grace to me. For that I am forever grateful to her. My father, on the other hand, was Buddhist, even though his spirituality was somewhat eclectic. He read the Bible often and was well versed in such Chinese classics as *The Analects* and *Chuang Tzu*, he recited the Chinese poetry of Tu-Fu and Li-Po and even Tennyson in English, but he also sat before a portable Buddhist altar at home and chanted sutras every morning. Thanks to his daily chanting, I learned some of the basic sutras by heart.

With Japan's defeat in World War II, he watched his world and its old values collapse right before his eyes. Unlike most of his Navy friends who perished in the Pacific, he survived the war and came home only to find his wife and daughter both dying of cancer/leukemia, which, I later learned, was probably an effect of the residual radiation from the atomic bomb dropped on the city of Nagasaki. Yet, he stoically accepted his fate; he never spoke negatively about the United States or the Western culture. Instead, he often spoke lovingly of his college English teachers. As a former officer of the Japanese Imperial Navy and academician, he was totally unprepared for the postwar survival race forced upon him, but he worked hard to support his family. At home, my siblings daily rebelled against our new stepmother, who responded to them with unpredictable emotional outbursts, and that, I knew, was tearing up my father. Understandably, he began his spiritual search for a reason to live and for inner peace as well. It was basically his Buddhist faith/philosophy that sustained him through those difficult years. When his children were young, he would often tell us some of the old Buddhist stories he grew up with, but he also encouraged us to pursue the Christian faith. Friendly and respectful interfaith dialogue was often exchanged at home. Between my sister and my father, I was exposed to the very best of the two great religious traditions.

I have thus learned to live comfortably between Buddhism and Christianity, between East and West. I always felt a great deal of respect for the simple, peaceful and mindful Buddhist way of life, and was attracted to their philosophy of non-duality, reverence for all living beings, and harmony with nature. However, I did not see any serious conflict with my own faith. I chose to remain Christian and went to seminary in Yokohama to study Christian theology. I then traveled to the United States for additional theological studies. I was ordained in 1972 in Seattle, Washington, and have since been in ministry in the United States.

I believe in God, but not in an anthropomorphic God like a nice Daddy in heaven who listens to every little prayer of his every child on earth. I lost such a naïve and simplistic notion of God long ago when I first learned of the horror and tragedy of Hiroshima, Nagasaki, Auschwitz and Dachau. In Nagasaki, only a hundred meters from the epicenter of the atomic explosion, was the largest Christian church in Asia. The heat of the blast literally vaporized the beautiful church along with its 8,500 members that morning. In Hiroshima, there was a group of church women holding a prayer meeting for peace by the bank of the Ota River when the atomic bomb exploded that sultry summer morning. They were devout and faithful women who did not believe in war and prayed for peace every day, but they were among almost one hundred thousand people killed instantly that morning. God did not even shield the faithful from the deadly power unleashed on August 6 and 9, 1945. I think God wept for all humanity for the collective loss of innocence. What happened that day has not only affected my health, but my faith also. I never really believed in prayers in terms of asking God for favors, although I believed in prayer as a way of discerning the will of God for me and for the world. God, to me, is not just an abstract concept or a set of rules or principles, but a living and loving presence whose essence is utter mystery. The God I have come to love is not He or She, let alone It. God is the foundation of all beings and the source of all wisdom. God transcends all beings, but is also immanent in all beings. God is Life and Love. I simply embrace the mystery of God and surrender my worries and burdens to God, who will continue to surprise me and keep me off balance so that I will never be able to claim to know God. This God whom I cannot know I love.

I have remained Christian also because I wanted to be loyal to the church that sustained me through the most difficult times in my life. The church has given me so much, and I have always wanted to give back to it all I could. I have always felt that my affinity with Buddhism and Eastern philosophy was a unique gift. It has helped me see the Western bias in the church's theology and practice more clearly. By "Western bias" I mean the church's imperialistic, or paternalistic, approach to its mission, individualistic orientation of its theology, dualistic redaction of the radically monotheistic religion of the Bible, and preoccupation with sin and guilt, etc., etc.

Also, there were a few issues about the Buddhist religion I was not totally comfortable with. The Buddha taught that in order to enter the peace of nirvana, one must renounce one's attachment to the world, which he said was all illusion, but I knew I could not possibly renounce my family, the church, or my commitment to justice and peace in the world. I could understand that love for family and for the poor could be more authentic once I had been freed from attachment, yet it would have required a lifetime of single-minded pursuit to reach that point. I often feel that Buddhism, especially Zen, is only for spiritual geniuses, not for ordinary people like me. Christianity, on the other hand, teaches us that Christ has done all that is necessary for our redemption. All we need to do is accept God's grace and live as forgiven and redeemed sinners. To me, that seemed to be the only way in which ordinary people like me could be saved. It is true that the Pure Land School, especially Shinran, taught us to rely on the Compassion of the Amida Buddha for salvation. Shinran's teaching of the so-called "Other Power" has paved a way for many people like me to be saved. His message is so powerful and so authentic that I sometimes wonder what I might have been if I had read Shinran before I read the Bible. By the time I read Shinran, however, my spiritual journey had already been founded firmly on Christianity. What Shinran taught me, therefore, simply reinforced the Christian belief of "justification by faith" over the "works of righteousness" scheme as a means of salvation.

The other aspect of Buddhism that I find a little uncomfortable is their seeming preoccupation with "inner peace." They do not exactly disregard the social evils and injustices, but they are so focused on their internal lives that they appear to be preoccupied with their own personal inner peace. I think it is generally true that Buddhists do not exhibit the same level of passion for social justice as they do for personal peace. It is also true that there have been many social justice activists in Buddhist history. Take Nichiren, for instance. I did not write about him in this book, but he was a great social reformer of the thirteenth century. He boldly criticized his fellow Buddhists for their spiritual self-indulgence and challenged them to fight for justice for all, especially for the poor and disenfranchised. He also challenged those in power to rebuild the nation based on compassion and equal justice as the Buddha taught. It amazes me that such a powerful prophet existed eight hundred years ago in medieval Japan and that his legacy continues to challenge the conscience of many today. There have been others like him throughout history, but there is no denying that the central pursuit of Buddhist philosophy is for enlightenment and inner peace, not for peace and justice in the world. They tend to be passive, submissive and deterministic about the injustices of the world, and I believe that is because of their basic inward orientation. Besides, if you believe all things in the world are merely a passing illusion, why devote your whole life to its reform?

Their inward orientation seems to be related to another issue, namely that of love vs. compassion. Jesus preached love, but the Buddha preached compassion. Love and compassion may seem similar, but I believe there is a subtle difference. I think love is more relational; it has to do with a commitment to relationships, while compassion has more to do with a state of mind. It is true that, in reality, there have probably been as many Buddhists as Christians who loved their fellow human beings and even sacrificed their lives for them, but the Buddhist teaching does not seem to emphasize love a as relational commitment because relationships are also illusion in their teaching. The subtle difference between love and compassion seems to have been amplified by the two different images of death. Jesus died an agonizing death on the cross for the redemption of the world, while the Buddha completed his long life and died peacefully. The image of Christ on the cross certainly has left an indelible mark on Christian understanding of love, just as the image of the Buddha's peaceful completion of life affected their core values of inner peace and quiet compassion.

Despite the fact that the inner life of Buddhists seems enviably rich and profound, my biblical-prophetic heritage informs me that our inner life and our social responsibility cannot be separated. Just as we seek to make the world a more peaceful and more just place for all its members, so we seek to keep our spirits free and at peace within at the same time.

I have cited some of the reasons why I still consider myself Christian, but that does not diminish my respect for Buddhism or Eastern philosophy. I do believe it is important to keep the two great religious heritages distinct, but we must also continue to be able to learn from each other. Buddhism has much to offer us today, particularly as we reexamine our theology in the face of pluralism and post-modernity.

Glossary

Ahimsa: The word literally means "no violence" or "no killing" in Sanskrit. It is an important notion in both the Buddhist and Hindu philosophies. Many Buddhists have practiced vegetarianism because their teaching prohibits killing or harming any living creature. Mahatma Gandhi, a Hindu, not only practiced a strict vegetarian diet, but also used the concept of ahimsa in his political struggles for Indian independence as the moral foundation for nonviolent civil disobedience. Martin Luther King, Jr. also led the Civil Rights movement inspired by Mahatma Gandhi's principle of ahimsa.

Amida: When Amida was a Bodhisattva, he vowed never to become a Buddha for himself unless he could bring into Nirvana all those who seek it with him. He became a Buddha by virtue of this vow. His name Amida has two Sanskrit roots — Amitabha (immeasurably radiant light) and Amitayus (eternal life). Historically, these two names correspond to the two aspects of the Persian creator-god Ahura Mazda as the lord of light and eternal life. The original Buddhism would typically emphasize that "the lamp of light" exists only within oneself, and thus teaches not to seek a power other than that which is in oneself for salvation. However, Amida invites people to place their personal faith and trust in his compassion, with which he vows to bring the entire world to the Pure Land. A possible early encounter with Zoroastrianism might explain the unique place of Amida worship within the Mahayana tradition. Shinran, the founder of the most popular school of Buddhism in Japan, called Amida's Compassion "Other Power" (Tariki) and taught his followers to rely on it completely, rather than relying on one's own "Self Power" (Jiriki) whose cultivation and refinement other Buddhist schools sought.

Atman, Anatman: The Sanskrit word atman denotes "self." The Buddha taught that "self" is an illusion. Thus, anatman (no-self) became an important concept in his teaching. Originally, the Buddha rejected the concept of atman because Hinduism elevated atman by identifying it with Brahma (The highest Being, Creator, God), which Gotama rejected. However, anatman was later interpreted by Chinese and Japanese Buddhists in a more moralistic sense as selflessness or even unselfishness. Japanese Buddhists, for instance, were taught to "die in individual selves (*sho-ga* in Japanese) and live in the Great Self (*tai-ga*)." In this case, the "Great Self" seems like Brahma, which the Buddha himself rejected. This is an example of the Indian metaphysical concepts reinterpreted in a more practical and moralistic sense by the pragmatic minds of the Chinese and Japanese Buddhists.

Bodhisattva: Bodhi means "enlightenment" and sattva "being." Thus, a Bodhisattva is a being who seeks enlightenment or one who is enlightenment itself. Abbot Takada Kōin of Yakushiji Temple in Kyoto once defined Bodhisattva as "one who strives eternally to find eternal truth." As one who eternally seeks true nirvana, a Bodhisattva is a compassionate teacher and companion in our journey to the enlightenment. Thus, Japanese artists have produced many statues and paintings of Bodhisattvas as the embodiment of compassion. Bodhisattva Avalokitesvara, for instance, is often portrayed as a benevolent female figure, as Virgin Mary is in the Roman Catholic tradition, and has many devotees throughout East Asia. A well-known sixth century statue of Bodhisattva Maitreya is also a feminine figure in deep contemplation. With her eyes half closed, she appears to be smiling mysteriously. There are other well-known Bodhisattvas, such as Manjushri and Samantabhadra. They all represent the idealized characterizations of those who seek eternal truth. In the Theravada tradition, however, the title Bodhisattva is reserved exclusively for Gotama Siddhartha before he became the Buddha.

Buddha: Ordinarily, Buddha is a title given to Gotama Siddhartha after his Enlightenment. (In Buddhist literature, Gotama is often called Sakyamuni, as he was revered as the Holy One of the Sakya Clan.) The Sanskrit word Buddha, however, simply means "enlightened or awakened one." Anyone who is enlightened or awakened can be called a Buddha. Therefore, there were many Buddhas before Gotama and after him as well. Mahayana Buddhism teaches that all persons are potentially Buddhas.

Buddhata: Buddha-nature or Buddha-heart in English. Buddhists believe that Buddhata is one's own true nature and it pervades in every being. Zen master Hakuin called waking up to one's own Buddhata "Kensho," and it is considered most important in his Zen training.

Hridaya: The Sanskrit word for "heart," both in its literal and figurative sense. The famous Hridaya Sutra's actual title is Prajna-Paramaita-Hridaya Sutra, meaning "The scripture that captures the heart of the Paramita wisdom."

Karma: The Sanskrit word for volitional action that passes into an unbroken chain of causality. To describe it, Buddhists often use the image of a rock thrown into a pond, creating ripples in all directions. The chain-reactions caused by an action are believed to continue throughout one's lifetime and beyond, but one's action is also a result of the karma of one's previous actions or of the actions of one's previous life. Thus, karma is often seen as an expression of Eastern fatalism: "Whatever happens to you is an inevitable result of your karma; you must accept it as your fate," many Buddhists might say. However, Buddhism simply teaches that one must "see clearly" the causality and interrelatedness of all things and move on with one's own life without blaming oneself or others for every negative experience and without elevating oneself or others for every positive experience.

Kwannon: A shortened Japanese name for Kwanzeon Bosatsu (Bodhisattva Avalokitesvara). When the Indian priest Kumarajiva translated the Sanskrit texts into Chinese, he rendered Avalokitesvara to Kwanzeon, or Kwannon for short (or Kuan-Yin in Chinese), as he understood Avolakitesvara as a combination of avalokite (seen) and svara (sound). Together it meant "one who sees the sounds." Hsüan-tsang, on the other hand, took the word as a combination of Avalokite (seen) and isvara (freely). So he translated it as Kwan-jizai (One who sees/knows freely). The name Kwannon gives the image of a compassionate one, while Kwan-jizai gives the impression of an omniscient one. While Kwazeon "sees" the weeping sounds of all the suffering beings, Kwan-jizai, the Wise One, freely knows what makes them weep. While Hsüan-tsang's translation Kwan-jizai is said to be linguistically more plausible, the popular devotion to compassionate Kwannon does not seem to diminish. The founder of Canon Camera, Inc., for instance, was a devotee of Kwannon, after whom he named his cameras in the hope that his cameras would take pictures accurate enough to "see" even the subtle nuances of the "sounds" behind the picture. That is what Kwannon is believed to do.

Nirvana: It literally means "without wind" (nir-vana). In Buddhism, it is the ultimate state of blessedness in which the wind of desires and passions has completely ceased. In other words, it is a state of complete liberation from the illusory attachment to things that have no substance. One can be truly spontaneous and autonomous only when one is completely liberated from all illusions. Thus, the Buddhists seek to reach the state of Nirvana as their ultimate goal through a lifelong series of renunciations.

Prajna, Vijnana: Sanskrit has two words for knowledge: prajna and vijnana. Prajna is intuitive, while vijnana is objective and analytical. Prajna is based on the integration of the seer and the seen, while vijnana is based on their separation. While vijnana is necessary in the world of senses, it only observes parts and does not see the whole. Buddhists seek to overcome the dualism of subject and object, being and becoming, "we" and "they," etc. Thus, they emphasize prajna, rather than vijnana. The Hebrew concept of "yadah" (knowing) is actually close to Sanskrit Prajna, while the Greek concept of "gnosis," from which the English word "knowledge" has come, is similar to vijnana.

Prajna-Paramita: This is an important concept in Mahayana Buddhism. Prajna means intuitive wisdom, as discussed above, and Paramita is the one who has reached the yonder shore. Therefore, Prajna-Paramita is the wisdom of those who have crossed the oceans of life and reached the yonder shore of wholeness and blissful peace. In other words, Prajna-Paramita is Perfect Wisdom that integrates all things.

Pure Land: According to the Pure Land School of Buddhism, it is an ideal place where all the obstacles have been removed for those who seek a spiritual life of true wisdom and loving-kindness under the guidance of the Buddha. In both Honen and Shinran, ordinary people's "rebirth" into the Pure Land by the Amida Buddha's Compassion was synonymous to salvation. Although it is spoken as if it is somewhere far away from this karma-bound world, it can also be said that it exists in one's heart.

Sanskrit, Pali: Sanskrit was the literary language of the Aryan tribes who migrated to India during the second millennium BCE. As Aryans became dominant in the Indian society, Sanskrit became the principal language of literature there. Gotama Siddhartha was probably not Aryan, but like many other literary people of his time, he probably read and wrote in Sanskrit. Most of the early Mahayana literature was written in this language also. As one of the Indo-European classical languages, Sanskrit shares common roots with modern European languages. Pali, on the other hand, was vernacular. The Theravada school preferred Pali as the language of their literature because Sanskrit was too closely associated with Vedic literature.

Sutra: The word sutra literally means "thread." It is a distant cousin of the English word "suture." In the religious context, it denotes a written text on religious or disciplinary subjects. It was called "thread" because it was meant to be as consistent and unfailing as a thread in the fabric of life. In other words, a sutra was to be understood as a spiritual "thread" of life for those who study and recite it. The earliest sutras consisted of short verses. They were probably written to be sung or chanted for the purpose of accurate memorization. However, some of the later Buddhist sutras became much greater in size. The Maha-Prajna-Paramita Sutra, for instance, consists of six hundred scrolls. Incidentally, maha, meaning "great," is a relative of the English "mega-." The Sanskrit "para-" is used roughly in the same sense as it is in English.

Tao: Tao is a Chinese word for "Way" or "Path." A more accurate rendition of the word may be "Nature's Way," for it is "the way it is" in nature. As such, it is akin to the Sanskrit tharthata (suchness). Taoism teaches that one must see and learn from Nature's Way without disruption by human ego.

Tao Te Ching: Strictly speaking, Tao Te Ching (Scripture on the Way and the Virtues) is a Taoist book commonly ascribed to Lao Tzu (544-463 B.C.), but because of its unmistakable influence on Chinese Buddhism in general, it has been widely studied by Buddhists also. Tao Te Ching's influence was particularly significant in the development of Zen Buddhism in China. Lao Tzu advocated Nature's Way and Inaction.

Yin and Yang: Yin and Yang represents an Eastern view of reality. "Yin" basically means shadow or shady side, and "Yang" sun or sunny side in Chinese. The Yin and Yang in a circle thus symbolize two primal opposing forces complementing each other and forming wholeness together. Those two opposing-complementary elements can be femininity and masculinity, passivity and activity, receptivity and creativity, dark side and bright side, etc. etc. As seen in the Yin and Yang symbol above, Yin and Yang are interdependent. Yin can be part of Yang and Yang part of Yin. The symbol also suggests that Yin and Yang are perpetually in movement.

Appendix 1

The Ten Ox-herding Pictures

by Tomikichiro Tokuriki

1. Seeking the Ox

尋牛

2. Finding the Ox's Traces

見跡

3. Finding the Ox

見牛

4. Catching the Ox

得牛

5. Taming the Ox

牧牛 五

6. Going Home on the Back of the Ox

歸騎 六
來牛

7. The Ox Forgotten

忘牛 七
存人

8. The Ox and the Seeker Both Forgotten

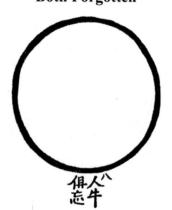

人牛 八
俱忘

9. Back to the Beginning

10. Entering the Village with the Bliss-offering hands

Appendix 2

Suggested Reading in English

Buddhist Texts:

Conze, Edward (ed.) *Buddhist Texts Through the Ages* (New York: Harper & Row, 1964)

Goddard, Dwight (ed.) *A Buddhist Bible* (Boston: Beacon Press, 1994)

On Zen Buddhism:

Sekida, Katsuki *Two Zen Classics – The Gateless Gate and The Blue Cliff Records* (Boston: Shambhala, 2005)

Chang, Chung-Yuan (ed.) *Original Teachings of Ch'an Buddhism* (New York: Pantheon, 1969)

Hakuin *The Essential Teachings of Zen Master Hakuin* (Boston: Shambhala, 1994)

Low, Albert (ed. com.) *Hakuin on Kensho – The Four Ways of Knowing,* (Boston: Shambala, 2006)

Hyers, Conrad *Zen and the Comic Spirit* (Philadelphia: Delta Press, 1973)

Suzuki, D. T. *Essays in Zen Buddhism, First Series* (London: Rider & Co., 1949)

Suzuki, D. T. *Essays in Zen Buddhism, Second Series* (London: Rider & Co.. 1950)

Suzuki, D. T. *Essays in Zen Buddhism, Third Series* (London: Rider & Co., 1953)

Suzuki, D. T. *Studies in Zen* (New York: Delta Publishing, 1955)

Suzuki, D. T. *Zen and Japanese Culture* (New York: Princeton University Press, 1989)

Suzuki, D. T. *The Field of Zen* (New York: Harper and Row, 1970)

On Shin Buddhism:

Bloom, Alfred. *Strategies for Modern Living, A Commentary with the Text of the Tannisho* (Numata Center, Berkeley, 1992)

Bloom, Alfred (com. and ed.). *The Essential Shinran – A Buddhist Path of True Entrusting* (Bloomington, Indiana: World Wisdom Press, 2007)

On Lao Tzu and Taoism

Mitchell, Stephen, Tran. *Tao Te Ching* (Harper Perennial, 1988)

Mabry, John. *God as Nature Sees God – Christian Reading of Tao Te Ching* (Rockport: Element, 1994)

For Buddhist Meditation Techniques for Christians:

Culligan, Kevin. *Purifying the Spirit, Buddhist Insight Meditation for Christians* (New York: Crossroad, 1994)

Buddhist-Christian Dialogue

Dunne, Carrin. *Buddha and Jesus - Conversations* (Springfield: Templegate Publishers, 1975)

Hanh, Thich Nhat. *Living Buddha, Living Christ* (New York, Riverhead, 1995)

Suzuki, D.T. *Mysticism, Christian and Buddhist* (New York: Harper and Row, 1971)

Ingram, Paul O. *Wrestling with the Ox* (New York: Continuum, 1997)